PRISON SAVED MY LIFE

LOUIS DOOLEY

Prison Saved My Life:
I Recommend It for Everyone
By Louis Dooley
Co-written with Heidi Gruber O'Very

ISBN 978-1-59387-290-8
ebook ISBN 978-1-59387-463-6
Code: B-PSML

Emmaus Worldwide
PO Box 1028, Dubuque, IA 52004-1028 USA
EmmausWorldwide.org

More than 17 million Emmaus correspondence courses have been distributed in prisons across North America since 1942.

"And now abide faith, hope, love, these three;
but the greatest of these is love."
~1 Corinthians 13:13

FOREWARD

I will never forget the day I met Louis Dooley. Working as a volunteer for the Missouri Department of Corrections at Potosi Correctional Center, I felt privileged to know many men who lost their freedom at a young age. Louis was no exception. He was young, good looking, athletic, and alive with a lifetime to live. One could not miss that he was, and still is, a people person who attracts others with his personality and vision. But what made Louis even more unique was his simple, sincere expression of his faith in our Lord Jesus Christ.

As time went on, I learned that Louis was serving a life term with 100 years. While he was active in the body of Christ and participated in the programs at Potosi Correctional Center, Louis was inconsistent in his attendance at the Bible studies in which I was involved. When he came, his interest in God's Word was always apparent, as well as his love for the other brothers who attended. As time went on, I gave him the nickname "Lazarus" because he would be absent for months and then suddenly appear again. It was not that he walked away from our Lord, but he simply got occupied in other programs and concerns.

Thankfully, the day came when Lazarus stayed, becoming an active and consistent member of the body. He took *Born to Win*, the first course in our curriculum of Bible studies, four or five times but didn't complete it. However, he finally continued on in the courses and showed promise as a teacher of others. He became an instructor for Set Free Ministries and remained faithful to that calling until he was transferred to another institution, having received an unexpected "out date," which you will read about in this book.

To his amazement and God's purpose, Louis was released from prison after serving just 15 percent of his time. He was now in his mid-30s. His new journey would be packed full of God's grace and mercy amid the many trials and testings that men and women experience when they get released from prison. The old man had been taken off. He put on the new man. The renewing process took over a life that at one time was without God or Christ, but which now lived in hope of glory with his heavenly Father.

Jobs were hard to come by. The death of his mom from cancer brought grief. A new marriage added to his responsibilities and concerns. A stepson created new challenges. I personally was praying that Louis would commit to being a part of Set Free Ministries, but I said nothing to him. After 3 1/2 years, he and his wife Julie caught the vision, and Louis committed to serve as a full-time worker with Set Free. I was delighted that our Lord would be so good to us.

This book highlights the key ingredients of God's dealings in Louis' life from childhood until the present. I trust that our Lord will use its pages to encourage and instruct all who read them in the thoughts and ways of God with men. Louis is certainly one of the elect in Christ in whom God has performed His miracle of grace. As you read of God's dealings in his life, enjoy and worship our Creator and the Redeemer of those who repent in God's presence and put their trust in our Savior and Lord Jesus Christ. To God be the glory!

Randy Gruber
A Disciple of Christ

PROLOGUE

Have you ever been at the end of your rope?

Have you ever felt the bottom fall out of your life?

Have you ever felt completely and utterly hopeless?

Have you ever felt rejected by this world—sometimes even by the very people who are supposed to love you?

Have you ever done something so horrible that the biggest punishment there seems to be is simply having to live with the knowledge that you did it?

Have you ever felt totally alone?

Have you ever wondered what's the point of this confusing and often painful thing we call life?

If you answered yes to any of these, YOU ARE NOT ALONE. I too have answered yes—emphatically yes—to each of these questions.

Have you ever wondered if there is really a solution to any of this:

- a knot to tie at the end of your rope
- a ladder to get back out of the hole
- hope
- acceptance
- forgiveness
- a companion to ease the loneliness
- a purpose...

If you turn on any talk show, go to any book store or scroll through any social media, you will find plenty of "solutions" for any of those. But do any of them really work? The onslaught of self-help fads is almost overwhelming. Isn't it true, though, that left to fix yourself, you will end up just as broken? You may even become better at pretending you are not. When no one is looking, what is the real state of your soul?

What if I told you that I found the answer to all of those questions? What if I told you that you, too, can find the hope, peace, forgiveness and purpose you so desperately want? Would you think it's too good to be true? I would. So instead of convincing you with arguments or theories, I'd like to share my story with you and allow you to judge for yourself. My story will resonate with you, make you uncomfortable, shock you, make you laugh and cry, but in the end it will give you hope. Ultimately, however, this story is about someone far greater than myself. Allow me to introduce you to—the Answer.

TABLE OF CONTENTS

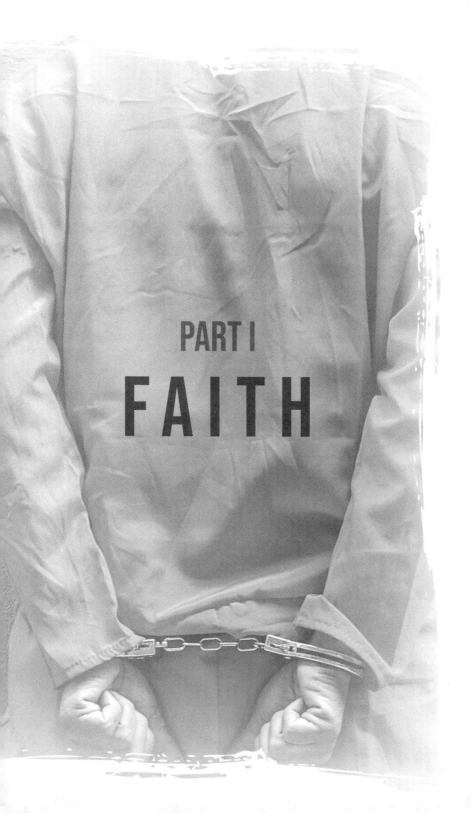

PART I

FAITH

CHAPTER 1

DEATH COMES IN A PAPER BOX

"Christianity was, and still should be, the religion of the open door."
~William Barclay
"The world is round, and the place which may seem like the end may
also be only the beginning." ~Ivy Baker Priest

"I'm gonna kill this dude. I gotta kill him. Don't nobody own me." The thoughts kept racing through my mind as the reality of my situation sank in and hope began to make its final exit.

I sat on my single bunk next to the catwalk in the day room of one of Clayton County Jail's modules. My head hurt. I felt agitated. I kept staring at the copy paper box at my feet. Stupid box. But it did hold the things that could help me feel a little bit normal again.

Normal? What the heck was normal about anything? My heart was racing. I looked around at the twelve other bunks out in the open just like mine. The steel tables bolted to the floor seemed to have more freedom than I felt at that moment. In the matter of a day, I lost my freedom, my family, possibly my future, and even my underwear. Nothing was between me and the dirty mattress but a flimsy orange jump suit. But the T-shirt, underwear, bag of chips, candy bar, Duplex cookies, and nacho chips stared at me from the box. To eat even one chip was to accept this gift, and even the greenest of inmates knew that nothing comes for free.

My leg began to twitch as I replayed the scene in my head. He had walked out of his cell, straight to my bunk and put the box at my feet. He wasn't a physical threat from what I could tell. Probably five-foot-seven, medium complexion, bald, maybe 22, and slim enough to look harmless. But looks are deceiving. There is no way he gave me that box just to be nice. I noticed that he lived in one of the cell-like rooms off the main day room. That could be helpful to take him out.

I sat straight up on the side of the bunk again and tried to breathe. The cocaine and weed that I had consumed that morning before showing up for court were wearing off. I needed a hit of something—anything to calm my mind which raged with a paranoia I had never experienced before.

As I helped supply the streets of East St. Louis with drugs, contraband, and anything else someone might want, I lived my life knowing every day could be my last. I was my own boss. I answered to no one, and because of that, I also made a lot of enemies. But out on the streets, I always had on my armor, which usually included at least one gun. But in here, I sat alone and vulnerable with no defense, no ally—nothing but a critical choice: take the box and be known forever as someone to be owned, leave the box and wait—who knew how long—to get the things in that box through normal prison channels, or take the box but also take out the giver and establish myself as someone not to be messed with.

I lay back down on my bunk. Around me, inmates mingled like it was any other day. I closed my eyes, willing myself to wake up from this dream. How did I get here? I had always been invincible when it came to the law. But now, I sat in a county jail, convicted of multiple major felonies and facing life in prison. Life. In. Prison. I was nineteen years old! How on earth would I be able to repeat this day over and over for the rest of my life?

I sat back up and ran my hands over my head. I let out a deep breath, opened my eyes, and saw the box again. If I was going to spend the rest of my life in prison, I would have to do what I had to do to survive and to make my life as comfortable as I could. That was it. I put on the socks and underwear. I ate some chips. I tasted the salty crunch and for a brief second could imagine I was eating those on my couch some random day before everything turned upside down.

A door slammed. I came back to reality, and my mind kicked into overdrive to make my plan. I wasn't huge on plans. But in this situation, I needed a basic idea at least. So I scouted the routines, the workings of this dorm. I noticed that many guys put up sheets over their cell openings for privacy. Since the guy who had brought me the box had a cell, this could be a huge advantage. I looked through the box again for anything that might be made in to a weapon, but there was nothing.

My plan would depend on the element of surprise and brute strength. I was strong, but I was not huge. I was stocky and young, and at the moment, more clean-cut than I had been in ages—all part of looking responsible for my trial. But in judging myself against him when he wasn't expecting it, I gave myself the win. I would either strangle him to death or bash his head on the toilet. Maybe a little of both.

Timing would be everything. I waited. Guys began to wind down for the night as they watched TV. I became nervous as everyone else began to relax. On the streets, I could spray bullets at my enemies from the safety of a moving vehicle. Here I was literally trapped in a box with nowhere to go if things went south. I had to be patient, stealthy even. Neither of those were my strong suit. I was a creature of impulse and adrenaline. I acted first, thought second. Here that would be deadly. As I watched the giver's cell, I noticed two men go in. I waited for them to come back out, but they didn't. This was bad.

I made my way to his cell, put my back against the wall, took a deep breath and rushed inside. The minute I was in the cell and saw the three men, I knew my plan was falling apart, even if for a split second the cocky kid in me thought about rushing them all at once. I saw their faces. Not a trace of worry was on any face. I felt the odd sensation of relief as I realized my plan was killed by three men sitting on a bed with Bibles in their hands. The guy who gave me the box had not even looked up from reading when I walked in. I couldn't move. The whole scene felt surreal. What the heck was going on here?

I stood stone still and just waited. Finally the man stopped reading and looked at me to ask, "Do you believe in God?"

I liked to talk, but he had managed to ask the one question I had little to say about. "I believe in evolution," I answered. All I knew about the origin of man was that we came from monkeys. Beyond that I had no belief system whatsoever.

The man didn't argue with me. He just handed me a red pamphlet with the word SALVATION on its cover. I looked down at it then back up at them. None of them said anything. They looked at me as if to say I was dismissed. For all my bravado, I felt like a boy among men in that room. I turned and walked out of the cell.

I walked back to my bunk. I was confused, frustrated, and a little angry at myself for backing down so easily. I felt so trapped. I had failed to take out that guy. What did that mean for me? I could only see one solution: kill myself. I would've given just about anything for a gun to end my life. I was lost—utterly and completely. I laid back down on the bed as the hopelessness washed over me.

I began thinking back over my life. I had been such a friendly kid. I had even excelled on the right path for years. But somewhere along the way, after life proved to be brutal and unfair, I became angry. Somewhere along the way, I had come to a fork in the road and changed course, the way a train switches tracks. That path had led me here. Did this path ever intersect with the other one again? Could I get back there or was this a dead end? It felt like a dead end.

I felt the paper in my hand and sat back up. I began to read it. It talked about how every single person is a sinner, deserving hell.[1] That no one, no matter how good they are, is good enough to reach heaven alone.[2] It talked about God the Father and God the Son, and that God sent His Son Jesus Christ to die on the cross for the sins of everyone.[3] I read on as it explained that salvation was available to anyone and everyone—even me—if I just believed that He died on the cross for my sins, then rose again three days later.[4] If I didn't accept Christ, I would stand before God and give an account for every bad thing I had ever done.[5] If I couldn't survive the court of man, how would I survive the court of God? Yet if I did accept that gift of His Son, a free gift with no strings attached, I would be forgiven.[6]

Forgiveness. That was not a word I had any use for in a long time. But I wanted off this track. I wanted out of this dead end. More than anything, I wanted hope. What this pamphlet said seemed to give me that out and that hope. On top of all that, I was tired. Tired of the pain of holding onto all the anger and hurt. Tired of the violence. Tired of me.

I closed my eyes and began talking to God. I said, "God, if You are real and if everything I read just now is real, then I am going to believe in You and accept Christ as my Savior. But the moment You show me that You aren't, I'm going to stop believing in You."

That was it. I waited, but nothing happened. No warm and fuzzy feeling swept over me. No angels appeared to me. Just the hum of the flickering light in the background as I fell asleep.

The next morning, the guy who had given me the box and the Bible tract approached me. He introduced himself as Jeffrey, and immediately I told him about accepting Christ as my Savior. "That's awesome, man. Praise God," he replied. "Just remember that this is a journey you will be on for life. Salvation is instant, but building that relationship with Christ will be ongoing. And man, it will be hard—very hard at times—but God will never leave you."

A few days later, I was approached by some Muslim men from MSTA (Moorish Science Temple of America) who told me that I had made the wrong choice by choosing Christ. They said, "Brother, that's a white man's religion! You need to proclaim your nationality. Christianity is just another way that white men continue to enslave black men."

I was only days into my new relationship with God, but I felt a question come to my mind. "My mother is white. Can she be part of your religion?"

The Muslim men responded emphatically, "No!"

Even in my limited experience with religion, I knew their religion was false. God had given me clarity that showed me just how present He was. I told them, "The God I serve created all of mankind and is not partial to any race."

They tried to convince me otherwise, but by the grace of God I stood my ground and parted ways.

During my stay at the county jail, Jeffrey began studying the Bible with me. In accepting Christ as my Savior, I had died to myself, and He made me a new creation.[7] I spent years in an environment where I could die at any time by any number of weapons. But death came in a paper box as one act of kindness showed me another way. It felt amazing to bury my old life and begin again with a life that may be imprisoned physically, but as free as one can ever be mentally and spiritually.

CHAPTER 2
THE RED BALLOON

"The way you speak to your child becomes their inner voice."
~ *Meg Meeker*

If you visited the nursery at Belleville Memorial Hospital on May 6, 1974, you would have seen all of the new babies and assumed that each of us were starting our lives fresh and with an equal chance at life. Babies hold nothing but promise, or so it seems. Reality, however, is that all of us are born with a balance sheet inherited by our parents and compounded by the circumstances into which we are born. For some, the balance sheet is filled with credits: mom and dad in a healthy relationship, a safe home, plenty of food, supportive family, and more. For others, the balance sheet is already so in the red that the debits seem almost insurmountable. To simply get back to a break-even place could take a lifetime.

I was born closer to the latter. That is not meant to be an excuse or complaint. It is simply the truth. But life is funny. Just like it can seem as if you have been born with the cards stacked against you, life can turn out to be full of miracles, too—miracles that take a life, turn it on its head, and make it all you dreamed of and more. My miracles wouldn't come until it seemed like my life was over. But I'm getting ahead of myself. First things first.

I was born Louis Fontaine Dooley Jr., to a white woman who was not yet even twenty years old and an African-American man ten years her senior. My mother was a kind, gentle, albeit headstrong woman who loved my father very much. Whether or not he loved her in return is hard to say. I never saw any affection from him toward her despite him living with us until his death. He had several other children by many women, yet he lived with us. Perhaps his choice to stay with her was his way of saying "I love you," but his violent outbursts toward her, as well as me, often sent a different message.

As a small child and well into my teen years, my mother worked at least two jobs, sometimes more, just to support us. She would go to work for the mayor of East St. Louis during the day, then work at Famous Barr at night. She woke me up at 5:30 in the morning to drive a half hour from our trailer in Edwardsville and drop me off at Grandma Velma's in East St. Louis by 6:00. Grandma Velma was my father's half-sister's grandmother, but her uncompromising love and care meant she was not just like a grandmother to me—in many ways she was the only true stability in my life.

I know my mother loved me, but I didn't really feel the love. I remember crying in the bathroom sometimes, just wanting my mother, but she couldn't be there. Or, I would pretend to be dead, like in a Bugs Bunny cartoon, hoping that it would make her stay home from work. But nothing ever worked.

The only upside to her hectic work schedule was that later she went on to work at Fairmont Racetrack, first as a third job, but later as a five-nights-a-week second job. She would drive to Fairmont to see if she was scheduled each night. If she had to work, I waited in the car and did homework. Someone would come check on me from time to time. When I got old enough, I actually went in and hung out, playing video games. I saw people leaving early, dropping their programs on the ground, so I picked them up. A new program sold for two dollars. I'd sell the ones left behind for one dollar and use the money to play video games or get a hot dog. It was my first attempt at being a business man. That, however, didn't make up for the loneliness I often felt. After Mom dropped me off at Grandma Velma's, Grandma Velma made me breakfast, and either I went to school or she would watch me. She also watched one of my half-cousins, Erica. Life at home with my mom in the trailer was often in stark contrast to life at Grandma Velma's.

Our trailer had three bedrooms, and was in a predominantly white trailer park. My mother would cook things like lasagna, and macaroni and cheese. Grandma Velma, on the other hand, lived in a small single family home in East St. Louis where she cooked things like neck bones, iced potatoes, greens, and fish her daughter caught. She was from Mississippi and had an easy way about her, though she was known to grab a switch from a tree if you didn't mind her. I remember walking with Grandma Velma to her church. Grandma was a small woman—proper and proud. She only wore dresses, never even a skirt. We had to walk through a park to get to her church. She would take my hand, and we would walk on through that park with gang members hanging out all around us. But none of them ever messed with Grandma Velma.

My mother would stop by between jobs for a brief visit, and we ate a treat like M&Ms or McDonald's. But then she had to leave again. She wouldn't be back to pick me up until 10 or 10:30 when we drove home to sleep, only to repeat the process again the next day. In some ways, the two homes represented the ongoing battle for acceptance raging within me. It didn't seem to matter that my mother and Grandma Velma were both loving, and in general, my mother was a happy woman. The truth was, the bubble of care that they both tried to give me could only shield me so much from what I saw at school and on the streets. I was growing up seeing that while I was both white and black, I couldn't seem to find my place to belong in either world.

One of my earliest memories is of standing in front of the doors to John Robinson Elementary School in East St. Louis, crying as my mother tried to coax me into the kindergarten class. I clung to my mother. It was not as if I had never been away from her before, but on this August morning I did not want her to leave me. She kept telling me, "I will see you in a few hours, Louis, and we'll go have a special lunch. I promise."

Being half Hungarian, my mother was a caring, nurturing woman, but her Sicilian blood gave her a tendency toward being stubborn and strong-willed. She was born and raised in East St. Louis, Illinois, which at the time was predominantly white. My father was born in Mississippi, but his father moved to East St. Louis, married another woman and had a daughter with her. My father was visiting his half-sister, and my mother was visiting her girlfriend who lived next door. When my mother was walking home my father saw her, pulled up next to her and started talking. Soon a relationship started. About a year later, I was born.

It was about this time that the city changed culturally. Sometime in the '70s, the white population started to move away as crime began to run rampant. Other ethnicities moved in. Growing up in East St. Louis was tough for me, not only because of the crime but because I was bi-racial. My skin was a lot lighter and my hair was much straighter! As I grew older, this became an issue with the other kids. *I was too white for the black kids and too black for the white kids.* I had to defend myself because of my looks. I also had to defend my mother because she was white in what was now a predominately black area. I started getting into fights at an early age. I learned early in life not to trust anyone. I had friends who would come over to play as if I was their best friend, but as soon as other kids came along they jumped up and left me sitting alone.

Things were not any different with white people. They did not want to have anything to do with someone who looked like me. My parents weren't married—my conception was merely an accident—so they looked at me as if I was a product of sin and therefore less than human. And the color of my skin often caused people to draw conclusions about me before they even knew me.

Yet, through all of this my mother was my rock. She began to teach me that there were bad people in the world but that there were also good people. She did not shield me from the fact that I would face ridicule and shame. Instead, she prepared me for it. She taught me the importance of education. In her mind, the only way to make up for my "disadvantage" was to become smarter than my abusers. Above all, she said that education would be the tool that I could use to put me ahead of everyone.

With the idea that education was my ticket out, I began learning to read, write, and spell better than everyone in my class. The more I learned, the more I was accepted. In sixth grade, I was selected to represent my school in spelling bees. I literally had time set aside each day to just study words, their proper pronunciation, and, of course, how to spell them. I got pulled out of class and would sit in the cafeteria alone with a dictionary and memorize lists of words. I liked the special attention. I liked the quiet of my study time. That was my escape from the madness because the reality in my world was that every day there was always another fight, shooting, or just something bad happening in the neighborhood. Some kids accepted me because of my talent in spelling, but others were jealous and used it as another reason to make fun of me. Despite this, I was able to make a few friends.

Spelling aside, the only fun I really remember having as a kid was sports. That's just what you did in my neighborhood. If you couldn't play ball, you were out! After school and during our entire summer breaks, we played the "big three": baseball, basketball, and football. This was exciting because I found something else I was good at and liked to do. It was the first time I was accepted among my peers. Life was good—at least for a while. After I graduated from sixth grade, my mother told me that I was changing school districts. I was shocked and more than a little upset. I had finally started to make friends, and suddenly I had to leave! My mother felt that I would get a better education and that it would take me away from all the crime if I went to a better school. This news felt like the worst day of my life. Grandma Velma still lived in East St. Louis, which allowed me to visit a few of my friends, but it wasn't the same as seeing them every day. Unknown to her, though, the decision she made in hopes of taking me out of the path of violence would be the one that led me straight to it.

* * * * *

I'd like to say that I didn't become a fighter or have a tendency toward violence until my world was turned upside down with the start of a new school in a much more white area of town. But the truth is that by seventh grade, I was already well-versed in violence and the concept that if you want something out of life, you have to take it—even if that meant taking it right out of someone else's hands.

I idolized my father, regardless of how detrimental that idolization was for me. It didn't matter that he was often incredibly mean, completely undependable, and one of the most serious men I've ever known. As I look back on my life and search for happy memories of the man that I tried so hard to emulate for so many years, only one memory comes to mind. I was around ten years old. My father was a Golden Gloves boxer, and one Sunday afternoon near my birthday we were watching boxing. A red balloon was lying on the floor, and for some reason my father hit it over to me. I hit it back. My father smiled at me and hit it back. We continued this banter for quite a while. Why we could never recapture that sort of connection, I don't know.

The first day of the seventh grade was crazy to say the least. I had to change classrooms for the first time. Everyone had a locker, and I had subjects I had never heard of before. I went from having writing, math, and black American studies to science, art, and home economics. That was the easy part, though.

For the first time I would be in a classroom with black students *and* white students. That was major! Now, I was the new kid with an afro, an accent, and a whole different style of dressing. I went from the city to the suburbs. In the city, it was baggy jeans and baseball caps worn backward. We were into the hip-hop culture. In the 'burbs, it was polos, straight-legged jeans, and dockers. We city kids wore our shirts untucked while the 'burb kids wore theirs tucked in. We had afros and jerry curls. The 'burb kids had high and tight cuts with hairspray and gel. It was all the important stuff that kids go through at that age, and I had it all wrong.

Needless to say, I started getting into fights all over again for being different. Just when I thought life was going to be easier, I had the rug pulled from under me. I started failing my classes. As far as my parents were concerned, that was unacceptable. First, it was my mother yelling at me, and then it was my father beating me. My father was a physically abusive person. That's where all the fight that was in me came from. I watched him beat my mother on many occasions, and felt the blows personally when my behavior was unacceptable.

I learned that when someone does something you don't like, you use physical force to make them do what you want. Despite the fact that my mother was kind and gentle, and taught me that being kind to others would get me far in life, I was drawn to my father's perspective like a moth to a flame. My father knew it was a dog-eat-dog world. If you wanted something, you had to make it happen. I learned from him that if an opportunity presented itself, you may or may not get another one, so you better take it—even if you had to step on someone else to get it. I saw my father get his way with people by being violent. I tried it, and it worked. I learned that most people don't want any problems, and that they would give in with just a little push.

Since the physical and verbal assaults were nothing new to me, my life went back to normal. I graduated the seventh grade and moved on to the eighth. I managed to make a few friends, so things got a little easier. I tried out for the basketball team but didn't make it. I was crushed. No one ever showed me how to play, so I understood why I was cut. Those kids had fathers and older brothers play with them, and they played on organized teams. In my neighborhood, we saw athletics as a way out—a way to have a great life. Little did we know that only a small percentage ever make it. Few of us possessed the natural gifts and skills to really succeed. The ones that did seemed to always get caught up in the street life with gangs, drugs, violence, or all of the above.

During that time, I still visited my old friends and played ball with them. I began to notice that some of them had started to change. They would talk about being in a gang and carrying drugs for other people to make money. They asked me if I wanted in on it, but I said no. However, saying no simply painted me as a coward, lame, and every other name in the book. I wanted to do it but was scared to death of my father finding out.

I occasionally saw my father smoke marijuana, carry guns, and bring suitcases of money home. I figured that since he was familiar with that lifestyle, he would be able to tell if I was involved. If he knew I was involved in any of those activities, that he would literally kill me. He knew that the future in that lifestyle was bleak and often short-lived. I believe my father wanted me to be better than he was and have better than he did. I never experienced much, if any, love from my father, nor saw much directed toward my mother. He was always serious and didn't play. That's what everyone said about my father, "Louis don't play!" That was a huge sign of respect because it meant that people feared him. And when people fear you, that's when you have power and control over them. Yet, I had so much peer pressure taking place in my life that it was making my head spin.

It is an interesting pull on a child to have parents with such polarizing philosophies. Years of effort put forth by my mother and Grandma Velma appeared to have little effect, while a single happy memory of a red balloon bouncing back and forth between my father and I—paired with an inborn desire to imitate the most prominent man in my life—took control of my worldview. But the choices I made in the coming years were not simply the result of picking one philosophy over another. They were the result of lashing out at life after a series of events—one after another in a domino effect—all started by that most well-intentioned choice to give me a safer school. But they came to a head with the violent end to the person I most wanted to be—my father.

CHAPTER 3
WHEN IT ALL COMES CRASHING DOWN

"God whispers to us in our pleasures, speaks in our conscience, but shouts in our pains." ~ C.S. Lewis

Despite the chaos and confusion that seemed to monopolize my junior high experience, I did manage to pass and moved on to the big leagues. That's right: high school. Everything that I had experienced in junior high was multiplied by four. The fights were bigger and more often, the classes more challenging, and the stakes for sports higher than ever.

I remember trying out for the freshman baseball team. I loved Roger Clemens and Kirby Puckett. For those of you who aren't familiar with those major league baseball players, one was a pitcher and one was a center fielder. I played both positions. They were amazing to me. Clemens was such a bulldog on the mound, never giving in to the batter, and Puckett exhibited his speed in center field and power at the plate. They inspired me to up my own game.

I went out for pitcher, but to make a long story short, I didn't make it. The coaches never even gave me a chance to bat, and where I grew up we could all hit. We played stick ball! We used old cut-off mop or broom handles for bats and tennis balls with the fuzz burned off to pitch. For our batting practice, we used the same bats but would pitch bottle caps. If you could hit bottle caps, you could hit anything. You can throw those things all kinds of directions. Playing with things like bottle caps also heightened your pain tolerance. You could easily get hit with one while batting or take a line drive if you were pitching, but that came with the territory. If you were scared, then you shouldn't have been outside anyway, or so we thought.

Yet all that practice and skill and toughness meant nothing when you aren't even given the opportunity to show what you really have. But that is the nature of sports. It wasn't enough to be a good hitter. They wanted the top in all areas. I understood that, even if I was disappointed.

Failing to make the basketball team in junior high and the baseball team in high school only left one option: football. This was my favorite sport, and easily my best. I was a physical kid, so football proved to be an excellent outlet for my energy and aggression. However, football season is later in the year, so I had to wait for tryouts.

In the meantime, I did the best that I could to work on my grades. But by my freshman year, I was so far behind everyone that I could only manage to get C's and D's. My parents, united at least on this subject, continued to stay on my back. But ultimately, it truly was the best I could do.

Finally, football season came, and when I made the team I was beyond excited. Then I found out that everyone makes it. That didn't matter, though. I knew I was good at football and felt that people would see that. I played defensive end and linebacker. I would have preferred to play tailback. I was five-foot-eight, 190 pounds, and could run through anything. Of course, I know now that is exactly why the coaches did not put me there. All I would do is try to run over everything. It didn't matter who it was either—my teammate or the opposing team. I had powerful legs but not quick ones. I was well-suited for the offensive or defensive line. I had a blast on the football field. I liked practice more than games, however, because they were every day and lasted a lot longer. It was my escape from all the peer pressure, violence, and even academics.

I got through my freshman year. At that point in my life, it was all about football. During the summer before my sophomore year, all I did was lift weights, do cardio, and start to prepare for the NFL. Like so many young boys, that was my dream. Growing up in the '80s, I wanted to be like Bo Jackson in football, Kirby Puckett in baseball, and Kareem Abdul-Jabbar in basketball. I tried my best to emulate them on the court and on the field, and hoped that one day I would be like one of them. In fact, all that football didn't take away from my love of baseball and basketball. I still played them whenever I had the opportunity. Sports, however, can break your heart as fast as they can build you up—faster actually.

One day during the off season, I was playing basketball and something happened that would change things drastically. I was running down the court on a fast break, and a guy came from behind me, trying to poke the ball out while I was dribbling. He bumped my right leg in the process. That knocked me off balance, and I tried to plant that leg to catch myself. I twisted my knee. The pain was so great that I shifted my weight to my left leg. I stepped wrong and twisted my ankle. I was in so much pain that I had to be carried off the court. I had broken an ankle before, so I knew what that type of pain felt like. This was easily just as bad, if not worse.

I was driven to the emergency room, and given an x-ray and MRI. The results came back even worse than I expected. I broke my left ankle and tore ligaments in my right knee. That was the end of my football career, I thought. I began rehabbing both injuries, and it wasn't going well. I was lazy and didn't do the prescribed exercises. I just couldn't get past the disappointment of not playing football. I felt that missing an entire season would cost me my spot on the team. Finally, I decided to do the shot put and discus in track instead of just sitting around. Little did I know that a sports injury was the least of my problems.

I found a new groove through participating in track. It wasn't football by any means, but it was something. Then one day after practice, I was walking home from the bus. As I approached my house, I noticed my mother standing in the doorway with a strange look on her face. I got to the door, and she burst into tears.

"What's wrong, Mom?" I asked.

My mother was sensitive so tears were not that uncommon. But then she dropped the bomb. "Your father was killed!"

Four words destroyed my life as I knew it. Four words caused more pain than any injury ever could. Four words changed everything.

I immediately ran to my room, slammed the door and started crying. It hurt so badly. It was worse than any pain I had ever felt. I laid on my bed saying, "God, I hate You." I don't know where that came from because while my mother was raised Roman Catholic, she had never really told me anything about God. I still don't know what my father believed. He definitely didn't live a godly life if he did believe. My heart was broken—torn to pieces.

Through all of the fear and beatings, I still loved my father with all my heart. I loved my father because of the respect he got from others. He was popular with everyone—a people person. He was charismatic and that drew people to him. Unfortunately, I never really got to know him that way. Yes, I was his son. But I had little interaction with him. He was rarely home, and when he was, he didn't want to be bothered. He used to beat my mother, stay out all night in clubs with other women, get high, and deal drugs. It didn't matter.

I desired to have a relationship with him, but now it was gone. I would never have a relationship with him. I just wanted to die.

The next day, I went to school. I thought it would help me put it out of my mind. P.E. was first period, and my friend Dave and I were the only ones in the locker room.

"Hey, man, you all right?" he asked me.

I paused, staring into space. "No. My father was killed yesterday."

Dave looked at me with suspicion. "Nah, man, he wasn't. Quit playing."

"I wish I was playing."

Dave sat down next to me, and we sat in silence. "You should go home, Louis. Straight up, man. Go home."

But I didn't go. The next class was history/government. There was a girl named Lynn in the class that I had a little crush on. Our teacher, Mr. Bosco, often fell asleep in the class, and we came and went as we pleased. I finally had to leave class because I couldn't put my father out of my mind. I walked out to the hall and sat down. I started crying. Lynn came out, and put her arm around me. The rest of the day is a blank. I missed the next few days.

In hindsight, I can see that I needed help to deal with the grief. I needed a release. And I needed my mother. We both needed counseling, but of course, that didn't happen. My mother went into her own little cocoon, and so did I.

I was originally told that my father was killed during a robbery at a car lot that he owned. For years, that is what I believed. Eventually I learned that, in fact, it had been a drug deal gone wrong. He had been shot by two men. Then his body was moved. If I could have, I would've sought revenge. But I couldn't. Both killers went to prison but were released after serving fairly short sentences. Ironically, they served less time for actually killing my father than I was sentenced to for attempted murder. But we'll get to that later.

My mother did her best to put on a smiley face, but I knew that just like my heart, hers was broken too. For her, dealing with the pain meant working two jobs. For me, I wanted to become just like my father. I know that sounds strange, but it's what made me feel closer to him—if I could emulate him in my life, I would understand who he was, and in some sort of way, know him. I thought it would give me a version of the connection that I so desperately wanted. All I had to do was figure out how to make that happen.

My first thought was to connect with my old friends and inquire about making some money. My father was a sharp dresser, and I had to be too. My friends welcomed me back with open arms. A few of them had worked their way up in the gangs and really wanted me to be part of it. But that would mean I would have to take orders from someone I didn't know and if I didn't carry through with it, it could cost me my life.

I told them, "No thanks!" I didn't listen to my parents, so why would I listen to some stranger I didn't even know? I learned not to trust people early in life, and I stood on that.

Because we had grown up together, I got hooked up anyway. I could get whatever drug I wanted whenever I wanted it. I chose marijuana since I thought it wasn't that bad. Now all I had to do was find a place to sell it. I knew quite a few people at school who looked like they might get high so I approached them. It took a few times but eventually they starting buying from me. My goal was to make as much money as I could. Even though I would never make it to the NFL because of my injury, I still wanted the NFL lifestyle.

I got high a few times myself, but it wasn't a big deal at the time. However, I was hanging around drug users, so my friends started to change. I would hang out with all kinds of different people. I found myself supplying most of my high school with weed. Football season came and went, and so did tenth grade. It was during the following summer that I really began smoking weed and found that I loved it. I got to the point that I couldn't sell it anymore. I would smoke all of it before even distributing it. This posed a problem because I wasn't making any money. I decided that I needed to make "real" money if I was going to ever really have nice cars, jewelry, and all the women. To do that I had to start selling crack cocaine.

A few people had asked me about cocaine, but at the time I was cool just dealing weed. A good friend of mine dealt crack, so I went to him to get some. He hooked me up and off I went. Before I knew it, I couldn't keep up with the demand. People were begging me for that stuff. By junior year, it was all about selling drugs and partying. I had a few friends who were girls. I sweet-talked them into doing my homework, so school was cool. I was barely passing, but that was okay as long as I passed. My mother was still depressed about my father and didn't know what was going on.

For as booming as business was, though, even the dark side has an even darker side. Along with all of the money and drugs came jealousy and violence. At that time, I had a couple of friends who were in the drug game, and we ran together. We would get into fights every weekend and most of the time we caused it. If we thought someone looked at us crazy or said something under their breath, we had enough reason to start a fight.

For me, business was good. I made around $400-$500 a week. One game we played was bank. We met in the park, and whoever had the biggest bank of money on them won the other person's money. That meant we literally went to the park in the worst part of East St. Louis with a couple thousand dollars in our pocket. Then we left with double that amount! That was pretty good for a high school junior.

But maturity wasn't my strong suit, so I blew it as fast as I got it. It was all about looking good and having fun. After all, I had plenty of friends now. What more could I ask for? Everyone wanted to ride along with me. And anyone who was going to be seen with me better look good too, so when I went shopping for myself, I also bought clothes for my friends. I liked being the guy people wanted to be with.

For some reason, during my senior year I just had a feeling something bad was going to happen. So when my mother and I took a trip to Alabama to visit my father's family for Christmas, I asked one of my uncles if I could come to live with him. I needed to figure out what I wanted to do after high school. He said yes. My father's family had always been encouraging for me. While my father may have withheld affection and attention, his family did not.

My mother's father was rather racist and always struggled with the fact that I was bi-racial. He never did accept my father. Thankfully the rest of my mother's family was very accepting. Her sister and brother were particularly kind to me. I was thankful that, for the most part, both families embraced me exactly as I was, and the feeling was mutual. In that way, I was fortunate because I was shown love by both my white family and my black family. Love was just love with no preference of color. But at this time, my father's side, removed from all the trouble back home, felt like an escape. It didn't hurt that they often complimented me on everything from how much better they thought my hair was to how light my skin was. I felt welcomed and accepted. They made me feel that I could be a better version of myself.

I went back home with my mother but immediately told her that I was going back down south to live with my uncle and his family. Her answer was, "No, you're not, Louis."

"Mom, I'm not asking you. I'm telling you. I'm going," I responded with all the attitude of a seventeen-year-old boy.

We fought about it until she realized that I would just go anyway. She finally agreed. I packed my bags, bought a bus ticket, and headed down south. I arrived at the bus station and called my uncle. "Hey! It's Louis. I'm ready to be picked up."

"Louis, hi. What do you mean you're ready to be picked up? Where are you?"

"I'm at the bus station. I came down to live with you like we talked about."

There was a pause on the line. He was shocked.

"I gotta admit, man, I never thought your mom would let you come. So when you asked if you could come, I didn't see the harm in saying yes." He paused again, thinking over the situation. "But okay, Louis. I'll come get you. You can live with me, but you gotta mind yourself. I don't want any trouble."

My uncle helped me enroll in school so that I could finish my senior year. A fresh start wasn't as easy as I imagined, though. It wasn't long before I started getting high and hanging out with the same kind of people that I had hung out with back home. One thing led to another, and I was selling drugs again too. I did manage to graduate high school. I also got myself kicked out of my uncle's house. School was over, and I had no plans for college. In the end, I went back home with my mother.

It is easy to look at this part of my life and ask what would've been if I had stayed the course in Atlanta. Easy to ask what could've been had I gone to live with him earlier and avoided getting into drugs. Would I have gone a different way? Would I have gone to college? Who knows. I guess it doesn't really matter at this point. I can see ways God was already looking out for my life, even though I refused to hear Him. The more He tried to get my attention, the more I ignored anyone but myself. But God is God, and He will be heard. If my life was represented by baseball, up until now I had been playing in the minors, but I was about to hit the major leagues. And He would be waiting when I finally struck out, and the game was over.

CHAPTER 4
GAME OVER

"You have sinned against the Lord; and be sure your sin will find you out." ~Numbers 32:23
"We get what we need...by walking through what we never wanted."
~Ann Voskamp

Gum. Just a single pack of gum. That's what I was buying the night I first stared down the barrel of a .38 revolver. It was 1993, and I was eighteen years old. It was a Friday night, and a popular rap group was performing at a local night club. As we drove by the club, we saw the long line waiting to get in. More importantly, the long row of women in line drew our interest. Since we didn't want to wait in that line, we figured we could just hang around and see if we could get some phone numbers, or even get some of the girls to get out of line and come with us. That was the plan.

We parked at my aunt's house just a few blocks away and walked over. We got across the street from the club, and one of the guys decided to stop at the gas station next door to buy gum. It made sense since we didn't want to offend the ladies with our breath. The gas station locked up when it got dark outside and served people at the window. Customers walked up to order, and the clerk would get whatever the person wanted and slide it through a drawer. As we approached the window, about five guys were standing around the window, though not directly in front of it. So we knew they weren't in line. I stepped up and ordered a pack of gum and waited for the attendant to get it.

One of the guys said to me, "Nice chain."

I ignored him. Then another one of the guys said, "Yeah, nice rings too."

I ignored him, as well. The attendant came back with the gum, and I paid him. We began walking away. Suddenly, I heard one of the guys say, "You need to come out of that jewelry."

I had between five and six thousand dollars worth of jewelry on. I stopped, turned around, and just stared at him. Out of nowhere, he pulled out a .38 revolver, and pointed it just inches from my face. I just stood there thinking that he was going to have to shoot me to get this jewelry. The other guy with us continued walking, but the guy with the gun told him to stop. He cocked the hammer. One of my friends slid between the gun and me. He raised his bag that held his cell phone (remember, in 1993, the massive cell phones came in a bag) as if he was going to hit the guy with the gun.

In that moment, it felt like time froze. I could see everything clearly. Suddenly, we heard a loud knocking noise. It was the gas station attendant banging on the big picture window with the phone saying he had called the cops.

The guy holding the gun said, "It's your lucky day. Get @#&$ out of here."

We started running away, but as we crossed the street, something hit me in the back of the head. It knocked me to the ground hard. As I fell, I saw the same thing happen to the other two guys with me. It was the cops! They patted us down and questioned us. I told them what happened, and they let us go. We got back to my car and pulled out every gun I had—about six guns. We drove around all night looking for those guys but never found them. It was their lucky night, as well.

* * * * *

When I got back to Illinois from Atlanta, I hooked right back up with my old friends, and started selling drugs. This time, I was serious. I wanted to make millions. I increased my supply and hit the streets hard. I started getting into it with other people who didn't like the fact that I was making so much money. I knew a war was brewing, so I needed some firepower. However, I did not like the idea of buying guns off the street because there could have been crimes committed with them. I didn't want to get caught with a weapon, and then charged with a crime that I didn't commit.

Within a few weeks of being home, I hit up a pawn shop and got the guns I needed. While I didn't buy guns on the street, I did not factor in witnesses to the actual crime I was committing. Almost immediately, the police contacted me and asked about a pawn shop robbery that my car was involved in. They asked me to come in to talk to them. I did so with the idea that I would just lie and say that I let someone borrow it. I figured that they would have to drop it. I was arrested for first-degree armed robbery for robbing the pawn shop at gun point. I used a fake name, stood in a line-up, and then they just let me go. I was invincible.

By now I was on multiple highs—not just from drugs, but also from a feeling of power and invincibility. I started getting into shootouts with people because of the money I was making, and because I did not respect the various gangs and their so-called territory. I was a free person living in America, and I could go anywhere I wanted. I almost got robbed more than once, and was involved in multiple drive-bys for doing just that.

Shortly before my nineteenth birthday, I was hanging out at a female friend's house. It was a safe house. She would let me stash stuff at her place and even sold drugs for me on occasion. Several of us were there when one of the dads of one of her kids came by. Despite a full house, he began abusing her, and we got into it. As we left, we exchanged words, angry at his nerve to go at her like that with all of us there.

He headed to his car, but to his passenger side. We assumed he was getting a gun because he hadn't ridden with anyone else. Immediately, the other guys started pulling out guns. I had no idea everyone had been sitting around packing that much heat. Thinking that we were about to be shot by him, we all began shooting at him. As the dust settled, I made sure that I hadn't been hit, and ran. I ran as far and as fast as I could—even over the highway before calling one of my best friends, Larry. He came, picked me up, and then we drove back to the scene.

Cops were everywhere, and I saw my car being towed. A witness said that car belonged to one of the guys in the shootout. Despite there being several guys all firing (resulting in the man being hit anywhere from fifteen to twenty times), I was the only one pursued. And since I refused to rat anyone out, I was the only one charged.

Logic would say that alone should have been my wake-up call. But the night of the incident I came home, and my mother asked me, "Louis, what did you do?"

"I ain't do nothing," I told her.

"You did something because your uncle in Atlanta just called me. State troopers came to his house after running the Georgia plates on your car. He gave them my number."

"I need to get out of here."

I went to a friend's house, got some money together, and flew out of the state. A few days later, I called my mother from a pay phone. She told me that a friend of mine brought a newspaper article to her at work. It named me in the story. She now knew what had happened. She urged me to get a lawyer, which I did. He asked if I had the money. Since I had the money, he recommended turning myself in and bonding out. I came back to town. My lawyer assured me that I had nothing to worry about because we would take the position of self-defense. They had nothing on me.

I refused to realize the severity of the situation, though. After I turned myself in and was charged with first-degree assault (which in any other state is known as attempted murder) as well as another first-degree armed robbery, I bonded out. All of those charges, and I still didn't stop. I continued to sell drugs and did whatever I wanted. I would stop at nothing to get what I wanted. My mother didn't know what to do. She begged and pleaded with me to stop, but I didn't want to hear it. I was consumed by the street life, and there was no turning back.

I trusted my attorney to get me off with the position of self-defense—especially since that's what it was. I definitely thought it was when it was happening. He prepped me for trial. He coached me on what to say on the stand, and we practiced a few weeks before trial started. I went to trial high every day, though. At that point, I had started smoking cocaine, and it blew my mind. I was gone!

After just three days of trial, I was found guilty. The jury recommended a sentence of life plus 100 years. I couldn't believe it. In reality, it was an excessive sentence for not killing anyone. If the crime had happened in the city, there was a good chance I would've been sentenced to about ten years. But the area of town where it happened had a gang problem. They were cracking down. It didn't matter that I wasn't actually part of any gang. They made certain assumptions and punished me based on that.

It would be easy to look back with a lot of resentment, but now I can clearly see how God allowed the misconceptions. It took stripping me of all hope in my life to see myself for who I really was: a lost man searching for something I was never going to find in the life I had been living. But that clarity would not come until much later.

I was handcuffed and taken into the back room. I remember sitting in a chair next to a guy I didn't know. I was crying uncontrollably.

The man looked over at me and said point blank, "Everything is going to be all right."

I looked him straight in the eyes and asked, "How is everything going to be all right when I just got life plus 100 years?"

The man didn't waiver. In my mind, though, my life was over. At the time, I didn't realize the potential for that man to be an angel extending to me the most valuable thing you can have when circumstances tell you it's all over: *hope*. My life wasn't over. It was just beginning.

PART II
HOPE

CHAPTER 5
REBOOT

"Therefore, if anyone is in Christ, he is a new creation; old things have passed away; behold, all things have become new."
~2 Corinthians 5:17 (NKJV)
"I find the great thing in this world is not so much where we stand, as in what direction we are moving." ~Oliver Wendell Holmes

It was not a typical day. I woke up in my own place, got high, showered, dressed for court, then left, never to return. It was even less normal to be told that I could be locked up in prison for the rest of my natural life. Stranger still was to stop taking drugs cold turkey without any help or encouragement, all while I began to grapple with my new reality.

Add to that the realization of the existence of an entirely other reality—a spiritual reality. If I continued as I was, I would not only spend my earthly life in a place that some would argue was its own type of hell, but I would literally spend forever in hell when I died! And while the news of salvation and the new idea of getting a second chance at life—both earthly and eternal—did carry some hope, it was still yet another bizarre layer to my already mind-boggling day. That day in 1994, atypical as it was, would prove to be the catalyst to a life I had never even imagined.

The moments after the judge ordered the maximum sentence he could possibly pass down are all a bit of a blur. Even my encounter with the man who was so sure that everything would be okay seems distant. Though when I recall it through the lens of the miracles that have occurred since that day, it is a moment forever marked in my mind. Shortly after being ushered out of the courtroom, I was taken over to intake at the county jail. Intake is much like you see in TV shows. I was told to take off all of my clothes, and was issued an orange jump suit and tennis shoes. They didn't even provide underwear. The rest of the intake process that most people associate with prison actually occurred when I moved on to Fulton Reception and Diagnostic Center, though I didn't head there for a month or two. That was where they did physical tests, as well as mental tests to assess any special needs or circumstances. That is also where they stripped me down, then sprayed me down to avoid bringing in any lice or whatever else they were worried about.

The other routine part of intake was being issued an inmate number. Looking back throughout my life, I can see glimpses of God reaching through the darkness, even though I didn't know it at the time. One example of that was in fact my inmate number. I thought my inmate number was based on my birthday because my birthday is 05/06/1974. But then I looked at others and realized that it wasn't based on birthdays. My inmate number was 506974—take 0 and 9 out and you have 5/6/74. At the time I remember thinking, "What if I get out in '09?" I did! I am not a numerology guy, but it did amaze me how my inmate number seemed to hold a clue of hope.

Clearly the flickers of hope were beginning to light through my life, starting on day one. The box, the botched plan, the tract with the salvation message, the knowledge that even I could get a fresh start. On that day, before I found hope in that little red pamphlet, I remember feeling so utterly hopeless, lost and full of despair. Initially, my encounter in the cell with Jeffrey and the other two at his Bible study had only compounded it. I had failed in my attempt to establish myself as someone who didn't take favors. As a result, suicide seemed like the only option. But then, those words in that tract started to redirect my thoughts. God worked on my heart and the rest might seem like history. But nothing is ever that simple.

I often hear people say things like, "Well, of course, people find Jesus in prison. They have nothing better to do." That is one of the single biggest misconceptions about prison, as well as prison ministries. Prior to that night in the county jail, my exposure to Christianity was minimal at best. I knew Grandma Velma went to church, but she never preached to me. My mom had a distant association with the Catholic Church, but again, never really exposed me to it.

Growing up, I had become angrier and angrier. I was a bi-racial young man living in the rough part of town. I experienced racism constantly. In fact, in high school, the majority of fights that I got into were racially motivated. As much as it seemed ideal to have a fair and balanced view of race since I was both black and white, it wasn't that way at all. I just didn't seem to fit anywhere. Despite the fact that both a black woman and a white woman invested in me and showed that love doesn't see in black and white, my experiences on the streets had hardened me.

I looked up to strong black men who stood up against racism and oppression. Rap groups like Public Enemy and KRS-One, which promoted the Nation of Islam, were some of my favorites. If you asked me what religion I would choose, I would've said Nation of Islam. Hands down. But here's the thing—truth is alive and active and powerful to change and to clarify. False faiths based on fear and hate simply cannot give the hope that I needed that night. I had been living an entire life based on vengeance, power, and money—taking anything I felt that I deserved. And it hadn't helped anything. In fact, it had sabotaged any future I could've had.

The next few days after I accepted Christ as my Savior, I was approached by the inmates who were part of Moorish Science Temple of America. Their recruitment efforts should've worked—at least on the old me. But in light of the faith I had found, I suddenly saw it for what it was: a religion with a severely limited god. It wasn't just that they told me that since my mother was white she couldn't be part of it, although that could've been enough. But it was more than that. I didn't want a god who could only help black people, and not just because my mother was white. We tend to simplify race. But the truth is, with all the inter-racial relationships over the centuries, we're all a little of this or a little of that. How could their god be THE God if his scope was so narrow? I'm sure they would answer that it is because there are different gods for different people.

In prison, it is a standard belief among many that Christianity is the religion of whites and Islam is the religion of blacks. So where did that leave me—a bi-racial man? Was I half Christian and half Muslim? But even that wasn't the biggest issue. If I was going to pledge my allegiance—in fact, my life—to God, I needed it to be a God who was God of everything. I wanted a God who could reach the beggar living in the gutter, as well as the king sitting on a throne. I wanted a God who could truly empower me to change.

That first night in the county jail, I knew for the first time in my life that I was truly lost. I no longer had any illusions of my own might or grandeur. *I saw myself for exactly who I was, and I needed not just a strong God but a merciful one. I needed a Savior.*

Race isn't the only deterrent to Christianity in prison. The other is actually a bigger one. Becoming a Christian is viewed as weak, and everyone knows that the most dangerous thing to be in a prison setting is weak. The reason Christians are viewed as weak is that while people often know very little of the actual Bible, somehow everyone knows the verses about turn the other cheek[1] and not seeking vengeance.[2] They also seem to think that Christians should somehow never do anything wrong. It is a favorite pastime of many to purposefully antagonize Christians with the sole objective of getting them to lose their temper or say something they shouldn't. Then they can label them as a hypocrite.

Intimidation is another reason. Among other things, one inmate will stand in front of a guy in the shower while he's naked just to make him uncomfortable. They will say they are hungry and ask the Christian to give them something to eat. This might not sound like a big deal, but in prison, food is not unlimited. They will often borrow items from Christians and never return them knowing that they won't fight back. To choose to be a Christian in prison is to accept a target on your back for all sorts of harassment. It is not something anyone chooses lightly because it comes at a high personal cost. That might make you wonder why anyone would choose it then. We choose it because the personal cost to ourselves is nothing compared to the price Christ paid. We don't reject the truth simply because it is difficult. Any ridicule we face isn't anything Christ didn't also face during his thirty-three years on this earth. He has never asked us to walk through something He did not also experience.[3]

Once I decide to do something, I do it. So I decided to be a Christian, and I committed to it fully. That didn't mean I didn't continue to get a lot of advice for how to survive prison. One group told me that since I was a young, nice-looking guy, I would have major problems when I got to prison. (This I already knew, but I listened anyway.) They said that in order to make it, I would have to prove myself to everyone by acting tough. They told me that I should find the biggest, blackest person I could find when I got to prison and try to kill him. This would prove to everyone that I wasn't to be messed with. I knew this was bad advice. My street sense told me this was a quick way to make enemies and could cost me my life. I decided that I would not listen to anything these people had to tell me. There were all kinds of views on what should and shouldn't be done when arriving to prison.

Since I was the only person in the dorm who had been found guilty, I was the talk of the dorm and even the dorm across the hall. This may seem odd, but county jail is usually for one of three things: either to hold someone awaiting trial for a crime they committed, or for someone sentenced to jail (not prison) time, or because a person is back from prison for an appeal or something else. As people talked about my case, everyone was comparing my crime to what his was and trying to figure out what was going to happen to them. I just continued to read the Bible and go to the various services that were available.

One evening, I went to a Bible study and was the only person who showed up. The guy leading the study said that since no one else showed up, would I mind telling him about myself. I said okay and began telling him about my past, what happened with my trial, and the amount of time I was facing.

He said that if the judge sentenced me to that amount of time (life plus 100 years), I would go to one of two prisons. One was the bloodiest sixty-seven acres west of the Mississippi, and the other was a new state-of-the-art prison built to house the most dangerous men in the state of Missouri. He proceeded to write down a couple of people's names. He told me that I should look them up and showed me which name went with what prison. I took the piece of paper and put it in my Bible. Honestly, I had no intention of looking up anyone. I remembered friends of mine telling me that if I ever got locked up that I should not look to anyone for help. They told me that was a sign of weakness and it would cause major problems. I believed that and decided not to ever try to look for help when it came to survival.

Over the next twenty-something days, I continued learning how to read the Bible and pray. I came across 1 Corinthians 10:13 in the King James Version. It really stood out to me. It said, "There hath no temptation taken you but such as is common to man: but God is faithful, who will not suffer you to be tempted above that ye are able; but will with the temptation also make a way to escape, that ye may be able to bear it." That was awesome! It spoke to me. There are no new temptations or trials out there. When they come, God will make a way for me to deal with them in a godly manner. I decided right then and there that I would stand on that verse FOREVER.

The day came to be sentenced. The judge had all the power to sentence me how he wanted. I went before him, and he sentenced me to every bit of time the jury recommended: life plus 100 years. I was taken away, and a few days later I got transferred to Fulton for about thirty days to be assessed. From there, I was transferred to prison. I didn't find out which prison I was going to until I was on the way there.

I ended up being sent to the new prison built to house the worst of the worst. I'll never forget the day I stepped off that bus. I was the only person taken there that day. What stood out the most were the huge fences and the razor wire. It was a sunny day, and the fences were gleaming. There were two layers of visible fence, which were also electrified. That was the scariest day of my life. I walked into the building, received a bag of clothes, and was told to go to housing unit 6-B, cell 13. I wasn't given any directions on how to get there. I guess they wanted to show me that my new life was going to consist of figuring things out on my own. I shouldn't expect help. At least that's what I got out of what they were doing.

I found housing unit six, and went inside. There was an A wing and a B wing. I went to the B side, and an automatic door opened to let me inside. What I saw was amazing! There were men everywhere. Music was blasting; people were playing cards, dominoes and all sorts of games. People were hanging out on the top walk and guys were standing all along the walls. People were on the phone. As I walked in, it got quiet. Everyone stopped what they were doing, and looked at me. I knew what they were thinking: fresh meat! I saw cell thirteen and headed straight for it. The door was open, and I went inside. It was obvious that there was someone living there, but no one was inside. The top bunk was open, so I threw my garbage bag of clothes on top.

I sat down in a chair and took a deep breath. That verse in 1 Corinthians came to mind, and I said, "Okay, God, here I am, and I'm standing on Your Word."

A guy walked into the cell and introduced himself as my cellmate. He was a small, skinny guy, and I didn't feel intimidated. "Where are you from?" he asked.

"East St. Louis. You?"

"Same. Man, that's a relief!"

I smiled because I knew why he was relieved. I was too, for two reasons. First of all, guys from St. Louis, Missouri, and East St. Louis, Illinois, don't usually like each other or get along (at least on the streets). Secondly, I knew that I wasn't placed in the cell with this guy because we were from the same town. This was a God-thing. I took this as God showing me that He was real and that He was there with me. I saw a Bible on his bunk and asked, "Are you a Christian?"

"Sure am."

I just shook my head, astonished at what God was doing. He had not only placed me in a cell with a guy from my hometown, but he was also a follower of His. I immediately asked him if he would show me where the chapel was and if they had church services. He agreed to show me around, and told me that they had services several nights a week. We sat back in our cell and talked for a while about how long he had been in, what he was there for, and about my situation.

The prison yard opened up for people to go outside, and we went for my tour. Unlike lower security prisons, this one did not allow inmates to roam the grounds at will. It was what was called a "controlled movement prison," meaning that inmates could only go from their cell block to somewhere else with permission or at designated times. This prison was different from anything I had ever seen or heard of. Of course, that isn't saying much because I hadn't seen or heard about many. There was a huge yard with a full high school-sized track with a football field in the middle, a sand volley ball pit, a softball field, horseshoe pits, and handball courts. On the inside was a full basketball court with two weight rooms. We made our way to the chapel where I met the chaplain and three of his inmate workers who were Christians. We had a chance to talk for a while, and I found out what days and times church services were. It just so happened that there was a service that night that I could attend. I was very excited.

Before we left the chapel, I applied for a chapel job because I had learned that everyone was given a job in the kitchen unless they found a different one first. That was another reason I was grateful for my cellmate's help. He told me that I had to find a job, or I would be placed in the kitchen. No one wanted a job there. The kitchen was the worst job a guy could have because it was dangerous. There were so many potential weapons. Plus the work was long, hard, and messy. I was eager to find a job quickly to avoid getting assigned to kitchen duty.

We left the chapel and decided to go walk the track. On the way, we passed the weight rooms. I looked inside, and I saw a guy who was huge! He was about 6'5" and looked like he weighed around 270 pounds. He was built like a statue. Immediately, I thought about what those guys in the county jail had told me. I thought that if I was going to try to hurt someone it would have to be that guy. Of course, I had no intention of doing that; the thought just crossed my mind.

We continued past and went outside to walk the track until it was time to go back in. Dinnertime came and it was nothing to write home about. Prison food is notoriously terrible, which is why so many guys become creative at making their own dishes back in their cells with snacks from the canteen. But that is a story for later.

After dinner, it was time for church. I was ready. I had on a brand new prison outfit, which was gray pants, a white t-shirt, and a gray shirt that looked like scrubs—the type you would see in a hospital—only these were dull. Nonetheless, it was the best that I had, and I wore it proudly. I took my Gideon Bible, and I was ready to go praise God!

We went to the chapel, and it was packed. The chapel itself was not that large. It was a rectangle-shaped room with the same cement brick walls as the cells we called home. It had a few slits for windows on the right-hand side, and a series of doors on the left-hand side which kept the chapel equipment. Since prisons have to accommodate all faiths, all faiths had the right to use the chapel. So the generic gray-walled rectangular room was converted to a Christian chapel by hanging

Christian banners. They were taken down at the end of the night. But the lack of ornate fixtures didn't deter anyone. People everywhere were shaking hands, hugging, and saying "Praise the Lord." I figured it was the Christian thing to do so I jumped right in.

To get to the actual chapel, we had to go through a common area off of which were a few offices, a bathroom, a small classroom, and a library. Once we got inside the chapel, there was still more handshaking, and now I could hear a piano. This was going to be my first church service being a Christian. I had been to small Bible studies at the county jail, but this was organized on a larger scale and included music and instruments. For being a guy who had never really been to church on the streets, this was a special experience.

As I turned to shake a few more hands, suddenly a hand the size of a catcher's mitt was in front of me. I looked up, and it was the guy from the weight room whom I saw earlier that day—the same guy that I thought I would try to hurt. I shook his hand as he said, "Hi, Brother, my name is Jacob Mills."

I almost fell over because in an instant I remembered that was the name on the piece of paper that the volunteer at the county jail Bible study had given me. I had not looked at that piece of paper since he handed it to me, but I remembered the name. And it was almost unheard of for an inmate to introduce himself with his full name. That was incredible to me. That was God showing me how real He was. There was no way that could be a coincidence. In that moment, I knew that God was real, and everything I had read in the Bible up until that point was real. In my heart of hearts, I decided that I would serve God until my dying day. I'll never forget that moment or that service. I felt God's presence like I had never felt it before.

Those first few months after my incarceration were both daunting as well as exhilarating. Yet for as excited as I was to turn my life around, and I knew that God had forgiven me, there was still one aspect that wouldn't be so easily corrected: my relationship with my mother. She had worked two, sometimes three jobs, just to create a better life for us and tried everything she could think of to give me the opportunities to avoid this lifestyle I chose on the streets. Despite all the hard work and the lack of affection from my father, she was a happy woman who always seemed to have a glimmer in her eye when she looked at me. She wasn't perfect—no parent is—but she was genuine. I knew she loved me, even if the ways she showed me were not always the ways I wanted her to show me.

When I was convicted of my crime, or at least when she understood what I had done, she felt total disgust and heartbreak. That glimmer in her eye was gone as if a part of her had died. While our relationship after my father had died had been rough, we still loved each other so much. I hated that I broke her heart and lost her trust. Once I became a Christian, I decided I would learn more about God and work toward regaining her trust. When you see crimes covered on the news, they always focus on the families of the victims (as they should), but families of those who are accused of committing those crimes suffer too. My mother had worked tirelessly and sacrificed so much to avoid the outcome that my choices led to. Even in those early days, I purposed to slowly but surely rebuild my relationship with her and to show her that it hadn't all been for nothing. I wanted to see that glimmer again.

Life in prison was rough from day one. Incredibly rough. My enthusiasm for God did not make me immune to the many challenges, pit falls, temptations and heartbreak that would be waiting for me in the days and years to come. What my new faith in God did give me was a way to handle it and work through even the most difficult times. I was twenty years old, and for the first time I was beginning to really live a life of substance. Prison wasn't just a wake-up call for me. It was a chance to start over. It was a chance for me to see myself and the world around me through the eyes of the One who made it all.

CHAPTER 6
SLICK-LEGGED

"If you begin, then begin well..." ~Bernard of Clairvaux

The first several days of prison were crazy. There was so much new information to absorb, and an entirely new culture to assimilate to in order to avoid crashing and burning. I did my best to take it all in. At times, my street smarts (or better yet, my street experience) definitely helped me navigate the twisted world inside a maximum security prison. All prisons can be dangerous at times. They can be a little scary and intimidating even for seasoned criminals simply because, unlike on the streets, there is nowhere to run or hide. You may avoid a man for a moment or escape a dangerous situation for a time, but if someone really has it in for you, you can't avoid them forever. You are literally locked inside a giant cage with him.

Maximum security prisons, like the one I was in, had another layer. The vast majority of inmates were either sentenced to life in prison, life without parole, or the death penalty. Bottom line: they had nothing to lose. One of the only things restraining the violence at times was the threat of the hole. The hole was solitary confinement. No visits. No recreation. No interaction for the extent of your stay. Most guys visited the hole at some point. Sometimes, two guys would be sent there to cool off for a few days after a fight. But most of the time, it was a significant punishment. If someone was sent to the hole, he usually had to work his way back up through the housing units.

Different housing units had different privileges. They covered everything from solitary and the spitters and throwers (men who, either because of mental illness or just sheer violent natures, were dangerous to be around, and known for spitting on others or throwing feces), to protective custody, medical, special needs, general population, and, lastly, those who through good behavior had earned special privileges like getting to help with special programs, etc. So there was an incentive to keep yourself under control, but for some, the incentive of special privileges was not a deterrent to revenge. Part of navigating prison life was knowing which inmates truly just did not care. Unfortunately, sometimes the only way to learn was the hard way.

When I arrived at Potosi, I was an infant in my walk with the Lord. I had been amazed at how much I had changed in just a couple of months, but I was still working to find the balance as to how much I should defend myself in certain situations. I knew I was supposed to be forgiving and avoid bad situations, if possible, but I didn't believe that I had been called to be a doormat.

Within a few days, I met a guy named Brock. We talked a little, and he suggested that we go out to the prison yard to get some air. I was apprehensive at first because I thought it might be a set-up. People do that in prison. They befriend you, get you to go somewhere with them, and then they take you to a place where their not-so-good friends are waiting. They try to scare you into hooking up with them. I figured I had to eventually trust someone, so I agreed to go but was very cautious.

As we passed people on our way to the yard, I felt someone "slick leg" me. "Slick leg" meant he grabbed my leg in a sexual way. I stopped suddenly, turned, and looked back. Out of all the people who had passed, one guy looked back. *That had to be the guy*, I thought. Otherwise, why would he look back? He had looked back to see my reaction. Brock noticed my pause and asked, "Hey, what's up?"

"That dude just grabbed my leg!"

I pointed out the specific guy I thought did it. "Oh yeah, that guy is one of the biggest 'booty bandits'" (homosexuals) in the prison."

I did not like hearing that.

"He actually lives in our housing unit. I'll show you which cell is his when we get back."

The whole time that we walked the track, all I could think about was how I had to deal with this guy when we got back. What was I going to do? Should I just let it go? I was afraid that if I let it go, it would escalate. I decided that I would confront the guy—put just enough pressure on him so that he got the hint to stay away, and that I wasn't interested. But I wouldn't hurt him.

When we got back to the housing unit, Brock showed me which cell was his. I immediately went to his cell and rushed in. I jumped on his back and wrapped my arm around his neck in a choking position. He struggled, but I held on for dear life. I didn't want to kill him, but I wanted to send the message to leave me alone. I wanted it loud and clear. While he struggled, I told him that if he ever touched me again I would take his life, though I hoped he didn't call my bluff. As he gasped for air, I could hear him saying that it wasn't him. In the moment, I didn't care. I eventually let him go and went down to my cell.

I hoped it was over, but it wasn't. As soon as I opened the cell door, two guys I had never seen before grabbed me. I struggled for my life. They didn't hit me or say anything. They just held on to me. After I was too tired to struggle anymore, they threw me into a chair and began talking to me. The guys were identical twins.

One of them just stared at me while the other spoke. He said, "Do you get that by going into that guy's cell and putting your hands on him, that you have a decision to make immediately?"

I looked at them confused. "I don't know what you mean."

The other twin pulled out a homemade knife and held it out to me. His brother continued talking, "That guy that you threatened is connected to a lot of people who are into some really bad things. Your life is in danger."

I was growing increasingly uncomfortable and nervous, but he continued. "My brother and I can't stand that these guys will take advantage of people when they get to prison, and we want to help people like you be able to fight back."

Wow! I didn't know what was going on! I had to make a decision right then and there. I looked at the brothers. I looked at the shiv. Should I take the knife and go take care of that guy, or should I stand on God's Word? It was one thing to stand up for myself. It was an entirely different thing to actually hurt or kill a man. Just days before, I had run across that verse in the Bible (1 Corinthians 10:13) that said that God wouldn't allow me to be in any situation that I couldn't handle. He would also make a way to escape. I decided quickly that I needed to obey God and not do what I really wanted to do in the flesh.

I told the twins, "I'm cool. I'm gonna just ride it out. But thanks."

"Ok. Suit yourself." They left my cell.

My cellmate was there, and he told me that they were friends of his. He apologized for how the whole introduction went down, but they had figured that I wouldn't listen unless they got my attention. That they did! I prayed and asked God to protect me. I told Him that I didn't want any problems. Nothing ever became of it. I thanked the Lord! But to my surprise, God took it a step further. He not only kept me from physical harm but allowed us to reconcile. We became cordial with one another, and years later facilitated several classes together. Doing it God's way had not only saved that man's life and possibly my own, it had also given me a friend.

Those first few months brought many challenges to my new faith—others trying to convert me to alternative religions, temptations to retaliate, and more. But I had made a decision, and I stood by it. I managed to start off on the right foot. It felt good. I felt empowered by God to be the better man—the man my mother had raised me to be. I wish I could say that after avoiding some major stumbling blocks in the beginning that I had it all figured out, and was a poster boy for Christianity going forward. But I can't.

It turned out that the line from that cheesy bumper sticker that says, "Christians aren't perfect, just forgiven," would become abundantly clear to me. I would learn that sometimes temptations come much more subtly and from places we don't expect them. I learned just how quickly my human mind could justify a sin with massive consequences. But I also learned that sometimes God's greatest mercies come to us in the form of getting caught and suffering the consequences of our choices because full repentance is the doorway to fuller blessings.[1]

CHAPTER 7
DIRTY URINE

"Be sure your sin will find you out." ~Numbers 32:23b (NKJV)
"God found Gideon in a hole. He found Joseph in a prison. He found
Daniel in a lion's den. Next time you feel unqualified to be used by
God remember this: He tends to recruit from the pit, not
the pedestal." ~Jon Acuff

After being a Christian for ten months and in prison for seven months, I still had my fair share of sin present in my life. By the grace of God, I managed to start out fairly strong, but that didn't mean I didn't give in to temptations like everyone else. I prayed daily for the Lord to help me overcome these sins, but some were more difficult to overcome than others. One of the hardest was smoking weed.

The first December that I spent at Potosi, we were having our first catered banquet for church. That meant food would be brought into the prison for us to eat in celebration of our Savior's birth. This was a big deal, and everyone was excited. If you have never tasted prison food—don't! Having food brought in was incredibly rare and a much bigger deal in prison than on the outside.

Earlier in the day, I went to a Christian brother's cell to talk to him about the banquet, and found him smoking weed. I was shocked! He was a brother who I really looked up to, and I never expected to find him doing that. He was just as shocked as I was. I went inside and closed the door.

"You want some?" he asked.

With little hesitation, I answered, "Yeah."

I knew it was wrong, but peer pressure got the best of me. We continued smoking for a while. We laughed about getting the munchies and "smashing" so much food later at the event. The banquet came and went. We had a great time of worship, fellowship, and feasting. I came back to my cell stuffed. I went over to that brother's cell, and we smoked some more before we had to lock down for the night. Lockdown came, and I went back to my cell. My cellmate was out of the institution at the hospital, so I had the cell to myself. I listened to music for a while and then went to bed.

Around 2 a.m. my cell door opened, and a guard stood in the doorway with a small bottle. He proceeded to tell me that I had to do a urine test. I couldn't believe it. How was it possible that I would be randomly tested after smoking all day? I got out of the bunk and peed in the bottle. I could have not peed, and the guy would've just come back in a few months. That would have been plenty of time for the weed to get out of my system. For some strange reason, I just thought that's what I got for not obeying God. I should take what I had coming.

The guard left, and I couldn't sleep the rest of the night. I knew I was busted. I felt horrible. I felt like such a hypocrite. And beyond the hypocrisy, I had worked so hard to build a solid and fulfilling life within prison. I had been blessed with a job in the chapel, and I was facilitating many programs in the prison. I was about to be accepted into the prison's youth program, which tried to help at-risk youth not make the same mistakes we made. I had to apply, and go through a tough interview to be accepted. I was working closely with one of the assistant wardens in a program, as well. I was involved in so many things, and almost every single one of them was contingent on good behavior.

One thing wasn't contingent on good behavior, and that was church. While I wouldn't be kicked out of church, how could I stand face-to-face with my Christian brothers? I was hurting inside because of my disobedience to God. To make matters worse, my mother was coming to visit me the next day, and I knew that I had to tell her. I knew that it would break her heart. I had treated her so badly for several years before I went to prison. I misused her trust, and disrespected her in every way. After I found Christ and made Him Lord of my life, she saw the change in me and began letting me back in. Now, it was like I had betrayed her trust again.

Before I faced her, I had to set up for church the next morning. That meant facing my brothers. I remember going to the chapel and as soon as I saw them, I burst into tears. I felt horrible! They wrapped their arms around me, and I told them what happened. As they listened, they assured me that I would make it through this and that they would be there with me all the way. That took so much of the burden away. I went to service and repented and asked God to please take the desire to smoke weed away from me forever—and He did.

After church, it was time for my visit with my mother. I still hadn't decided if I was going to tell her what happened. My mother was an emotional and compassionate person. She would cry about anything. It didn't matter if it had anything to do with her or not. Usually she would visit with my step-father, but that time he hadn't come. So it was just she and I. I got into the visiting room and couldn't even sit down before she asked me what was wrong.

Here we go, I thought. I broke down crying and told her what happened. While I was talking, I noticed something that I had never seen before. She wasn't crying. There was no way possible that she could not be crying. I would have bet my life that she would be crying more than me. Nope. Not a tear.

What happened next was just as amazing as her not crying. She looked me in the eyes and told me that it was going to be okay and that

WE would make it through this. I'm still as shocked now as I was then. How did she do it? How was she able to be so calm and comforting? I felt as if I could shoot straight to the moon! God really worked through her to help me in that situation. God is SO good! That was the best visit we ever had. I felt a connection with my mother that I never had before. I left the visiting room feeling tremendous relief. However, forgiveness—as precious as it is—does not mean an absence of consequences.

A few weeks went by, and the results came back positive (of course). I was escorted to segregation where I spent two weeks for my punishment. That wasn't the end though. I received my disciplinary sheet, and it was written on all over the front and the back. Almost every bit of space was taken up on the form. I was removed from every program that I was in and wouldn't be able to reapply for years, if ever. I felt like everything in my life was taken away—like I was going into prison again. I got out of segregation, and the whole prison knew what happened. All of the non-believers made fun of me and my faith. They called me a hypocrite and said that my God wasn't real. I was sad and furious at the same time. I had to allow God to rebuild what I had broken. In an effort to help with that, I decided to tell everyone my story about smoking weed, and to give God the glory for Him delivering me from the desire to smoke.

Slowly but surely, everything was restored back to me. I was able to get back into all of the programs that I had been in before, but it took about two years. I even made it into the youth program and in a short while became the secretary for the group.

That was my first real experience with God dealing with me and my sin. It reminded me of the story of David and Bathsheba.[1] God had blessed David as a king and given him so many gifts. Despite that, he gave into his human impulses and sinned against God with Bathsheba, and orchestrated the death of her husband. David was shown his sin and repented,[2] including penning an entire Psalm on the subject of repentance: Psalm 51. However, even with the repentance and the forgiveness, there were consequences. David's son, who had been conceived as a result of that adulterous relationship, died.[3]

Sin has consequences for us all. The fact that I was serving a life plus 100 years sentence was proof enough that there were consequences for sin. But those sins I had committed before coming to know the Lord as my Savior. Clearly, weed wasn't nearly as "big" of a sin as what landed me behind bars. But I felt the impact so much more personally because I hadn't just impacted myself. I had caused the name of God to be mocked and that hurt more than anything.

But there was another aspect to that situation that was different than before I became a Christian. This time, I felt convicted of my sin like I never had before. The turmoil I felt was real and raw. It was the loving chastening of God the Father via the Holy Spirit. Whom the Lord loves, He corrects.[4] In essence, the entire situation, from the random drug test the one night I had smoked weed, to losing all of those programs and having to work my way back over the next two years, was all proof that I was in fact a son of God now. He wasn't going to look the other way for blatant sin. Yet, unlike my earthly father, who would pound me when he got angry with something I did, everything in that situation had a certain buffer of grace. I saw in the eyes of my mother and the embrace of my brothers just how cleansing true repentance is. Transparency, while at times difficult, led to deeper, stronger relationships with those who mattered most to me.

In the story of David and Bathsheba, the death of their son wasn't the end of the story. After marrying David, Bathsheba gave birth to Solomon, who became the heir to David's throne, and was the line through which Joseph, Jesus' earthly father would come. David was also part of the direct lineage of Jesus Christ through his son Nathan.[5] Repentance led to blessing—for David and for me.

How awesome that while God is holy and must address sin, He is also the One who provided the Way for us to be reconciled with Him again through the work of Christ on the cross. While we should not sin just to see more of God's grace,[6] it is liberating to know that God is so in tune with our lives that He will help us live the best life we can for His glory. In a weird way, everything that happened as a result of some dirty urine helped solidify my faith. Not only did I serve a loving God, but also a just, holy, merciful, and all-knowing God. With each hurdle that came my way—whether of my own doing or someone else's—I saw just how big my God, THE God, really is.

CHAPTER 8
FOR WHOM THE BELL TOLLS

"And as it is appointed for men to die once, but after this the judgment, so Christ was offered once to bear the sins of many. To those who eagerly wait for Him He will appear a second time, apart from sin, for salvation." ~Hebrews 9:27-28 (NKJV)

"It's all in how you finish..." ~NCIS

Consequences—in our current culture that can almost be a dirty word. Few people actually believe they deserve consequences for their choices—at least if those consequences are negative. Morals and ethics have become increasingly relative and negotiable. Whether or not people want to admit it, though, sin is sin and God has to address all sin. For many, they answer not just to God but to man too. For some, the consequences for their actions are deadly. In the state of Missouri, they come in the form of execution.

According to Wikipedia, fifty-four men were executed while I was incarcerated at Potosi Correctional Center. I personally knew forty-nine of them. Since my release, nineteen more who I knew personally have been executed. I have known sixty-eight people who were put to death for their crimes.

When I first got to prison, I learned that the prison where I was incarcerated housed death row and actually executed people. Over the course of being in prison for only a year, I saw six people executed. The first person was a guy who I played handball against. I got to know the other five at various times throughout the year. That meant I knew every single one of the six people who were executed in the first year. Imagine being not even twenty-one and seeing six people you spent time with put to death. For each one, I knew it was happening as I laid in my bunk at night, and I knew they wouldn't be there tomorrow. It didn't matter where you came from or what you saw on the streets. Execution was a different beast altogether. It was calculated and looming. And in the instances when it was a close friend—it was devastating.

Nothing prepares someone for his first experience with living in a camp where executions occur. The person scheduled for execution was taken out of general population about a month before the actual execution date. He would then be placed in protective custody. That was just like solitary confinement. The person would be in a cell by himself for twenty-four hours a day, seven days a week, awaiting execution. When the date came, the entire prison was locked down after the evening meal (around 6 p.m.). The prison rented two movies to be shown over the prison's institutional channel. The person was brought to the execution chamber (a room in medical where we would see the doctor) and then executed by lethal injection around 12:00 a.m.

We remained locked down for breakfast, and a brown bag with fruit and a box of cereal was brought to us in our cells. My cellmate, myself, and countless others were praying for the person. I didn't know the circumstances in each person's case. Maybe he was guilty and deserved to die. That wasn't my decision to make. My prayer—our prayers—were for the person to accept Christ as his Savior. I remember sitting up all that night watching TV, and listening to the local radio station to see if the person was executed or if he was given a stay of execution. A stay would occur if the courts decided that there was more information that needed to be reviewed in the case, and then the state wouldn't execute the person. But a stay was not to be for him. He was executed. About a hundred yards from where I lived, a person's life was taken.

I went to lunch that day and saw hundreds of people with their prison identification cards covered with a homemade black stripe across them, signifying the death of "one of us." There was also complete silence in the chow hall—something that only happened when someone was executed. The solidarity among the inmates was amazing. I had arrived to that prison just a few months after there had been a major race riot. One couldn't tell that a riot ever happened because everyone was together in one accord.

The prison staff immediately began to panic and started asking people to remove the covering on their IDs. Everyone I saw refused. One guy told the guard that they cover their badges when an officer dies, and that we should have the right to cover our IDs when an inmate dies. The officer still said no and that if they didn't uncover their IDs, they would be handcuffed and taken to administrative segregation. The inmates didn't uncover the IDs, and the officers cuffed them and took them away. Literally, a panic ensued and tensions ignited. I personally saw over fifty people locked up. It was crazy!

I thought, *Wow. This is what life is going to look like for me forever.* It was eye-opening to me as to just how precious life really was.

Years went by and many more executions took place. There was another one scheduled and like most of the others I had gotten to know the guy. His name was Big Mike. He was one of the older inmates who worked in the recreation department. He was "the man." Everyone got along with him. When I say everyone liked him, I mean *everyone.* He was likeable and a fun guy to be around. He always joked with everyone to make prison more bearable. Just like all the other inmates who were executed before him, his time was up. Word spread like wildfire that Big Mike had gotten his execution date. We anticipated that any day the prison would be locked down, and they would come to get him.

One day, I was in the dorm of my housing unit when about ten white shirts (higher ranking prison staff) came into the wing. They headed straight to Mike's cell. They told him that they were there to take him away, but before they would, they were going to let him say his last goodbyes to people in the dorm. Wow! I had never heard of this happening before. A hundred people lived in one dorm, but not everyone was there. People gathered around Mike to give him a handshake and hug. I was one of those people. As I hugged him, I told him that I would be praying for him, and that God loved him and would forgive him of everything he had done if he placed his faith and trust in Christ. I knew that Mike wasn't a believer and that he was associated with the Islamic religion. Myself and many other Christians prayed for Big Mike until he was executed. We never knew if he placed his faith in Jesus Christ but were confident in knowing that he had heard the truth.

This happened several other times over the years—situations where I was able to hug someone goodbye who was being taken away to be executed. These times continued to help me remember how precious life really was and that death awaits everyone.

Executions were stressful and saddening, even if it was a stranger being taken. When it was a friend, though, it was truly life-changing. Within the first couple weeks of arriving to prison, I got a job in the chapel as a porter. I had to clean up and set up the chapel for the various services. There were Islamic, Wiccan, Nation of Islam, and Catholic services to name a few. We had one chapel where all groups met, so I had to get things ready for each service. There were a few other chapel workers too. One of them was named Jay. Jay was an older guy with a short white beard and glasses. He was the chaplain's clerk. Jay was from a more rural area of Missouri and seemed to be a genuinely nice guy. He really helped me to learn how to do my job well. He was patient and easy to get along with.

Over the months, "Brother Jay," as I called him, and I became close. Jay became a mentor to me, helping me learn my way around

God's Word. He had a lot of godly attributes. Brother Jay was the type of guy that one would wonder why he was in prison. I usually wasn't interested in knowing a guy's crimes, but sometimes it just came up. I would hear people talk about other peoples' crimes and, sometimes, their own. I already knew that Brother Jay was on death row. Over the course of time, I learned that Jay was a Vietnam vet who had done several tours. Unfortunately, he battled PTSD. He snapped one day and killed several state troopers, which had led to him being sentenced to death. But even knowing what he had done, it didn't change my view of him. I had learned that sin is sin in God's eyes, and that it's all punishable by death. If we are in Christ, then we are a new creation.

One day, I was around a few brothers, and they were talking about people on death row and their time coming up to be executed. Jay's name was mentioned. Years had passed by that time, and Jay and I were very close. He was like a spiritual father to me. He always encouraged me to keep God first in my life and to never waiver in my faith. He helped anyone in need. A few people on the list were executed, and Jay's time was quickly approaching. I remember when the state of Missouri gave him an execution date. He came to us and let us know because he didn't want us to hear it from anyone else.

Jay said to us, "Please pray that no matter what happens that the Lord's will be done. I'm at peace with this."

I wasn't at peace with it. I really wrestled with it. I had grown to love Brother Jay and didn't want to see him go. I told him, "I'm not ready for you to go. I'm having a hard time with this."

Jay responded, "Louis, we will have an eternity to spend together one day. What's important now is for you to keep your eyes on the Lord."

His answer helped calm my mind and heart. Shortly after, I really wanted to talk to Jay again about his date coming up and to ask him for something I could have to remember him by. That was a heart-wrenching conversation. How do you ask someone you love—who is going to be executed—if he would give you something to remember him by? I asked, and he said he would give me something.

Days went by after that, and I knew that there was still hope. There was always the chance for an appeal to go through or his sentence could be commuted. One day, a number of us were at the youth group and word came that the staff had just escorted Jay away. It was customary that when a death row inmate received an execution date that the staff would take him to isolation for safety reasons. Myself and a few other brothers were crushed. I had to leave the group early. When I reached my cell, I found a picture book of tractors on my bunk. Jay had given it to my cellmate and asked him to give it to me. My heart was broken. My brother was gone to be executed.

The night that he died, I laid awake on my bunk watching the minutes go by, praying for grace for him. As the time came and went for it to be completed, I knew the life in his earthly body was gone. It was one of the toughest days of my life. God's grace was strong for us that day, though. That was the only explanation as to why we made it without losing our minds. Brother Jay was a large part of the foundation of our church. He could not be replaced. Comfort for me came in the hope I had that one day I'd hear that old bluegrassy country voice again in heaven.

As 1 Thessalonians 4:13-18 says,

> But I do not want you to be ignorant, brethren, concerning those who have fallen asleep [died], lest you sorrow as others who have no hope. For if we believe that Jesus died and rose again, even so God will bring with Him those who sleep in Jesus. For this we say to you by the word of the Lord, that we who are alive and remain until the coming of the Lord will by no means precede those who are asleep. For the Lord Himself will descend from heaven with a shout, with the voice of an archangel, and with the trumpet of God. And the dead in Christ will rise first. Then we who are alive and remain shall be caught

up together with them in the clouds to meet the Lord in the air. And thus we shall always be with the Lord. Therefore comfort one another with these words.

That knowledge was truly the only comfort to be found in the situation.

For a long time, I wondered why Jay chose to leave me a picture book of tractors to remember him by. It seemed like such an odd choice. But eventually a theory came that tractors were commonplace where he came from. They reminded him of home. I think maybe he was leaving me a message to not be too sad. He was just finally, truly going home.

CHAPTER 9
GROWING IN CONCRETE

"O my soul, thou art capable of enjoying God, woe to thee if thou are contented with anything less than God." ~Frances de Sales
"The work we do is only our love for Jesus in action. If we pray the work...if we do it to Jesus, if we do it for Jesus, if we do it with Jesus... that's what makes us content." ~Mother Teresa

Living in a place that was so centered around death, whether the crimes that landed the guys there or the death of the inmates themselves, the true fragility and brevity of life was so crystal clear in ways that it wasn't on the streets. It was a strange dichotomy, though, because in another sense, if one didn't keep busy doing something worthwhile, the days and even the life could seem endless and mindless. In any life, having a purpose is critical and that is rarely more true than when serving time. Most inmates at PCC would never see the streets again, so trying to wait until release to fully live was pointless. For some, the idea of living a full life in prison may sound impossible. I guess it's like anywhere, though, in that purpose and fulfillment have far less to do with *where* you are as it does with *who* you are.

I was a new man who now worked for the Creator of the universe. I had found my calling and no amount of heavy steel doors, bars, or restrictions could deter me from being all I could be for God. I would do my best and face the challenges head on. Sometimes I would get knocked down, but adversity seemed to only challenge me to push harder, think differently, pray more. Life in prison while serving the Lord taught me to grow even in the most unlikely places.

Shortly after getting a job working in the chapel, I found out that we would be passing out Christmas cards to the entire prison population. I thought that it was going to be so cool—having the opportunity to bless other inmates with a gift that would help them bless their families. Wow, was I wrong! We separated the different boxes of cards and counted all of them. We found that there weren't enough of the specialty cards to give one to everyone. We decided to place the cards that we didn't have enough of in the window and let the men select one from among the varieties. We blocked the door of the chapel with a table, and we stood behind the table and passed out the packets of cards we had put together. The inmates had to show us their ID card, and we checked them off the copy of the prison roster.

That was the first problem. The inmates quickly started calling us "the cops" (which wasn't good) because we had a roster that only the staff had access to. They also cussed us out because we would only give them one packet. They didn't understand or care when we told them that we wanted to make sure everyone got a packet. If that wasn't bad enough, I was singled out and called every name in the book by a big-time gang member. He called me out (wanted to fight me) in front of about seventy prisoners. I couldn't believe it. I remember thinking that this was it. After being in prison for about seven months, I was about to lose my life. I couldn't just let this guy "punk" me in front of all those guys. It would be all over the prison that I was a coward and then everyone would try me. I quickly thought about my commitment to Christ, though, and that I didn't want to be the same person with the bad behavior that had landed me in prison in the first place.

My brother Jay whispered in my ear, "Just ignore him and let him talk."

I took his advice and continued passing out cards. That was the toughest morning in my incarceration to that point. By God's grace, no one said anything to me about the incident. I found out years later that the gang guy had been murdered in a drive by shooting shortly after his release.

Encounters like that only fueled my desire to improve myself. I wanted personal resources for handling life that went beyond the violence and hustling that had characterized my life on the street. So when a group of volunteers came into the prison a few years later to start a chapter for an organization called Toastmasters, I was interested. Honestly, I was interested in every program the institution provided. I had never heard of Toastmasters but knew that I wanted to look into it. Programs like Anger Management and Positive Mental Attitude kind of speak for themselves, so I knew what they were about. I remember going to the first meeting and hearing that it was about public speaking, which was something that I was interested in and had hoped to be involved with someday.

The volunteers were attempting to start a chapter at the prison, and we needed twenty paid people to make that happen. They were able to cut the cost down to around $50 a person. Because of the indigence of people in prison, though, it took us over a year to try to get the money. Unfortunately, we were unable to get chartered. However, during that year, we operated as a Toastmaster chapter.

The volunteers brought in the beginner kits that had the first five speeches in them. I was overwhelmed with joy to begin to learn to speak in public. The first speech was an icebreaker. Since I was used to sharing testimonies in church, I figured that one would be pretty easy. Well, I was right—and wrong. I had the content down for the most part, but I was terrible with body language, eye contact, and pretty much everything else. They actually timed us, and then critiqued us when we were finished. While a person would be giving his speech, everyone else would be writing down every time he said "um," "ah," "you know," and any other idiosyncrasies. We were all a mess!

As the weeks went by, there was an inmate who was pretty good, named Marcus. He was clearly the competition. I had my sights set on beating him in every aspect of speech writing and presentation. We competed against each other well. Marcus always won but not by much. I learned so much during that time. Marcus was such a great driving force to push me to be my best. He was a natural. But in prison, as in life in general, a strong façade is not always real.

As we were nearing the end of our sessions (due to lack of funds), something terrible happened. It was a normal day, and I was in the chapel working. Suddenly the institutional activities coordinator bolted out of her office. Then prison guards were running down the hallway. That was pretty normal. I assumed either someone was fighting, trying to kill someone, or any number of other things. Usually they would place the prison on lockdown when things like that took place, but that time they didn't.

About an hour later, the activities coordinator returned, and I saw that she had been crying. That was strange. She was a tough person who was usually strict, and even mean at times. The chaplain came in and told us that Marcus had committed suicide. He had hung himself with his bed sheet from the end of his bunk. I couldn't believe it. A heaviness came over me. As far as I had experienced, Marcus wasn't a believer. He was a good guy who was smart but usually stayed to himself. Marcus was also on death row. I don't know for sure what motivated him, but rumor had it that his execution date was coming up, and that he told his friends that he refused to let the state kill him.

It was a sad day. I had gotten to know Marcus, and we enjoyed competing against each other. That, however, was not what grieved me the most. I was most grieved because I had not been more intentional about talking to him about the Lord. I had been so focused on "winning" the speech competitions that I had forgotten to interact with him on a more important level. It was a wakeup call that helped me understand the importance of spreading the gospel in any and every situation. We just do not know how much time we have with anyone.

Marcus's suicide really impacted me that I needed to become bolder for Christ. I didn't consider myself a shy guy, by any means, but being a Christ-follower in prison wasn't popular or easy! One of the biggest challenges I initially encountered was people questioning my faith. I would get bombarded with questions about the Father, Son, and Holy Spirit. I had only been a Christian a few months before that line of questioning started. Needless to say, I didn't have many answers. That intimidated me, so I chose not to intentionally have conversations with nonbelievers about Christ.

There were plenty of other brothers who could have those conversations. They knew the Bible like the back of their hands. I justified my lack of evangelism with that for several years, but finally I learned something in a service that changed everything for me. I was at a Bible study when someone taught that no one person knows everything and that it's okay to say I didn't know something. Wow! That was awesome and liberating. It was shocking and refreshing to hear that it was okay to not know everything, and that I could still share what I did know. All of the nonbelievers had always said that if I didn't have the answers then my faith wasn't real. Now, I heard that if I didn't know the answer to something, simply tell the person that I would research it and get back with them. That would give me a reason to return to the person for further conversations.

I thought, *What a great idea!*

This new information was transformational for me. It empowered me to really do what I had been feeling God wanted me to do. I wanted to share Christ, but Satan had me believing the lie that I was inadequate and wasn't smart enough. I began praying for the courage to approach others with the gospel of Jesus Christ. I went to a brother who I knew prayed diligently and told him that I planned to go to the prison yard and randomly witness to others about Christ. I asked him if he would pray for me while I was on the yard. He said yes.[1]

The next morning at 8:00 a.m., we were released to recreation. The brother and I prayed together before I went out, for as Edwin Louis Cole said, "Prayer in private results in boldness in public." I remember being nervous yet confident, which was really weird because it didn't seem like those two feelings should go together. I went out to the track and saw a guy with his shirt off and tattoos everywhere. He even had a swastika on his forehead which told me that he was in the Aryan Brotherhood and didn't want to be approached, let alone with the gospel. Still, I went up to him and asked, "Do you believe in God?"

I know that wasn't very original, but it was all I had come up with before heading out to the yard. He looked at me and answered, "No," and continued walking the track.

What a victory! He no doubt had a shank on him and could've lashed out on me because I wasn't Aryan. He didn't, though, and I was happy. I went to the next person and then the next. I spent the entire two hour recreation period witnessing to others about Christ. No one committed their life to Christ while I was with them, but seeds were planted. I was not out to force my faith on anyone. If there was one thing I knew, it was that we all have a choice. No one can make anyone choose God sincerely. It has to be the work of the Lord and the decision of the individual. But I still needed to be the faithful messenger. My faith in Christ grew tremendously that morning. It made me "fearless" when it came to approaching random people to have a conversation about Christ.

I went back to my housing unit and told Walter the conversations I had. We rejoiced and thanked God for His protection and the bold spirit He gave me.[2] Walter asked if I would go with him to witness to others that afternoon, and I said yes. He and I went out. I would talk to the people, and he had his Bible open, reading to the people what the Bible said. It was the most beautiful experience I had my entire incarceration. I can truly say that Walter and I tasted what the early disciples experienced in Christ's day.

For every uplifting experience like that, there were also stories of disappointment like that with my friend Matt. By the time I met Matt, I had come to the point where I really enjoyed getting to know people and witnessed to new people who were coming to prison. I found that relationship evangelism was a more effective medium to sharing the gospel than just randomly walking up to people every day. I was learning how to disciple and mentor people. There was something that stood out about a particular new guy, Matt.

We met on the basketball court where I met most of the guys. He was a peaceful person who didn't really get into the normal disputes that most guys did on the court. (I've seen guys get their heads busted, lives threatened, and even stabbed.) I really liked that about Matt. As we got to know each other, I found that he had been raised in the church all his life but never had a real relationship with God. We would get together several times a week, and talk about life as it pertains to God and about the Bible. We had some really good conversations. I had become comfortable enough with him that I was going to ask him to give/rededicate his life to Christ. I knew this would be a little risky because it could push him away from me, but I was willing to take the chance.

I'll never forget the day. Matt and I went outside and sat down at one of the tables. We talked a few minutes, and then I asked him, "Have you ever thought about establishing a relationship with God through Christ?"

Matt looked me dead in the eye and said, "Louis, I know the type of man Jesus wants me to be, and I'm not ready to be that man."

I wasn't expecting to hear that. He was correct; he knew all about Christ because we had talked about Him extensively over the months. That was my first encounter with someone who knew the truth but didn't want to accept it. I wondered if it was because he felt God couldn't forgive him. That was a common thing inside prison. Or, was he afraid that if he gave his life to Christ he would endure harsh ridicule from fellow inmates—something else that was prevalent in prison. I never got to find out because Matt decided that he didn't want to talk about God with me anymore. That really hurt! I felt terrible and thought that I pushed him farther away from God.

As time went on, I came to understand that every man has to make a choice to accept Christ or reject Him. I also learned that God wanted me to continue to talk to others about His Son and to ask them where they stood. That was no easy task, being in a maximum security prison, but it was one I gladly took on for Christ.

While trying to be an ambassador for Christ was certainly a primary focus of mine throughout my incarceration, I was not immune to the day-to-day basic needs and interests that come with simply being human. I continued to love sports. At one point, I even hosted a show on the prison's TV channel, called Trash Talk. A buddy of mine named "Shakey" joined me as we videotaped everyone during rec. We talked sports and explained rules for various sports. We also talked about the performance of guys playing the sport—sometimes good, sometimes especially bad. The guys loved it because it was fun and silly, and of course, most people wanted to find themselves part of the show. We hosted that two times a month. I also played a lot of sports. Pretty much any sport could be fun to me as long as it was active and competitive.

Sports, however, wasn't my only interest. Food was, as well. I remember the first time that I saw a "prison pizza." I was sitting in the day room, and I saw my cellmate walk out of our cell with what looked like a pizza. It was round and had sauce and toppings on it. Yep, it was definitely a pizza. I was immediately upset because I saw him giving half of it away to a friend of ours, and he hadn't given me any.

My next thought was, *Where did he get a pizza from?* (They didn't sell pizza in the canteen.) *Why does he have it right out in the open?* (I thought that a staff person must have given it to him which was against the rules—big time!)

I went over to him and said, "What's up?"

He asked, "Do you want some?"

"Heck, yeah!"

As I looked closer at the pizza, I saw that it wasn't a REAL pizza but some made-up concoction. I tried a bite and didn't like it at all. The crust was ramen noodles, and the sauce was chili. The toppings were sliced beef salami and jalapeno peppers. It looked good but tasted terrible! Since I liked everything the pizza consisted of, I decided that I needed to try to make one, but I had a few other ideas of what to use. I decided to also check around and find other dudes to get some pointers. They suggested using graham crackers to mix with the ramen noodles to make the crust taste better and give it better consistency. My cellmate had used saltines which made the crust pasty and dry. After experimenting with many different topping ideas, I became a "prison pizza master." One of my favorites was tuna pizza. Tuna pizza had tuna, ranch dressing, onions, bell peppers, cheese, sour cream and onion chips, and hot pickles. Still makes my stomach growl.

Our creativity didn't end with pizza. After all, what is dinner without dessert? After bugging the canteen manager for months, they finally began carrying instant cheesecake mixes. All a person needed was a little butter and milk, and voila! They sold squeeze butter and instant milk already, so we were roaring and ready to go. The only thing we had to figure out was how to refrigerate it. We didn't have refrigerators, but we had small coolers that we could fill with ice. This would have to suffice. I bought one, made it, and it turned out okay. I was kind of disappointed, though, and decided that I wouldn't buy another one—or at least I thought I wouldn't buy another one.

One morning after coming from the canteen, I happened to see a few guys around a table with a few cheesecake mixes on the table, along with a few pints of ice cream. I knew one of the guys well and decided it was cool to be nosy. When I reached the table, I saw that they were using ice cream to mix with the instant cheesecake mix. What an idea! They made a cookies-and-cream one and a strawberry one. Then we really got inventive. We bought candy bars and crushed them up. We put them inside or used them as toppings. We also changed the way we cooled them. We cleaned out our small trash can and filled it halfway with ice, then put the bowl inside. We covered the can the rest of the way up with ice. They would actually freeze in about three hours. We were in heaven with our new frozen treat.

Thankfully, we didn't keep all of our creativity for food and sports. Everything we became involved with we sought to fine-tune or enhance. Two such programs were Y.E.P. (Youth Enlightening Program) and I.C.V.C. (Impact of Crime on Victims Class). Both of these programs were so important in their own ways.

The Y.E.P. was created to help at-risk youth (ages 12-18) who were in group homes, juvenile detention centers, etc. The program consisted of twenty inmates who shared their past histories or a psychological prison story with the youth. The past history was just that: sharing what he had done that led him to prison in a seven-minute talk. The psychological prison story was focused on what mentally bothered him while he was incarcerated (for example: one roll of toilet paper per week, when a family member died he couldn't go to the funeral, etc.).

At times, it was a volatile and hostile environment. Each member of the group had to be screened and voted in unanimously. The first time I applied, I was turned down. Every member of the group really had a passion for helping those kids avoid making the same mistakes we made. Believe it or not, only a couple of Christians were even involved.

We had to practice our talks and craft them in a way that they could understand. The past history took place in the morning session. These were designed to show the kids that we were just like them before we went to prison. We painted the picture of how one petty crime could lead to major crimes, which could lead a person to prison. We were strict with the kids. They couldn't talk, they had to sit up straight in their seats, and pay attention. An inmate played the "bad guy/bully" role. A few people also played the "good guy" role. We would get some really hard-headed kids. I was once in one kid's face about him pulling his pants up and putting on a belt that I gave him when his brother ran up behind me to try to attack me. Luckily another group member grabbed him before he jumped on my back.

The afternoon session consisted of a few of us sharing what really bothered us inside the prison. That was to show them that prison wasn't just about the physical issues but also the mental. Most people can handle the physical things in prison—the fights, the food, etc. The mental part is what really breaks a person down, and most people don't handle that well.

We also had a letter writing program associated with Y.E.P. If any of us really connect with a kid, we could write to them. They just had to let their counselor know who they wanted to write. They would send the letter to the prison's activities coordinator, and they would screen it. If there was nothing in the content that we couldn't have, they would give it to us. In turn, we would write a letter back and give it to the coordinator. After they screened it, they mailed it to the kid. I had quite a few of the kids who I wrote to over the years. They all just kind of dropped off after the years went by. I prayed for them and hoped they would get their lives on track. I would always tell them about Jesus. That program was truly a blessing for me and many others. *We actually had an opportunity to give back and help the world that we tried to destroy.*

Unfortunately the program ended abruptly. I heard through the grapevine that a similar group to ours in a different prison had an incident with an inmate and a student, so the Department of Corrections decided to shut down all the groups across the state. We were disappointed. I believe that we were really making a difference, but that was just how things went in prison.

The I.C.V.C. class was created to show the "ripple effect" of people's crimes. Most people think that there is only one victim in a crime, but there are always more. That class was designed to talk about nine major crimes, and to look at the effect that they had on the other people around the victim and the communities. The class was mandatory, which doesn't go well with people in prison. I took the class willingly, and it really helped me to understand how my crimes affected so many others! I believed in it so much that I signed up to become a facilitator.

We selected the crime in the curriculum that we committed, and shared about our crime and how it affected others. (There was always a staff person who helped with the class as well, but we always asked them if they would step back and let us take care of everything.) We watched a video that was related to that same crime. After each chapter, there was homework that had to be completed. We went over that in class too. I saw many guys go to Ad-Seg (jail inside jail) for not doing the homework or not attending class. After all, that class was mandatory!

There were many guys who came but wanted to just disrupt the class. We facilitators would ask the staff person from the prison to let us handle those people. We asked the guys if they would be respectful to us and not disrupt, and we'd respect them by not calling on them in class. They simply had to be quiet and not go to sleep. However, in many cases, by the second day they would interact with us like everyone else.

There were two crucial aspects to this class. One was on the second-to-last day, when everyone had to bring a picture of someone they loved. Most people were reluctant because people's families were not to be played with. That was taboo in prison. It was mandatory, though, so everyone did it. If someone missed one day of class for any reason or didn't do an assignment (such as bringing in his picture), he would have to take the entire class all over again! No one wanted that! They gave the pictures to us, and we randomly selected a few to talk about as it pertained to the last chapter, which was on murder.

We changed it up, though. Before the class started, we got a white sheet and had a guy lay on it like he was dead. We drew an outline on it, and then cut it out. We used it for the last chapter. We placed all the pictures face up on the sheet. That was to help everyone visualize what it would look like if their loved one was a victim. But we took it further.

We randomly grabbed a picture and briefly acted out a crime involving the person/people in the picture. We would do that for every picture. We didn't hold back on the crime or the acting job. Boy, did it work! I never saw so many "tough guys" choked up and with tears in their eyes. Some guys got fighting mad.

Despite all of that drama, the last day of class was still the most impactful. Actual victims from other states came in, and each one told their graphic and horrific stories: vehicular homicide, rape, assault, and several other crimes. After that day, every one of the men would be sobbing. Many men approached us about becoming facilitators. In most cases, they were accepted and trained. What an impactful and important class. It was truly a privilege to be part of I.C.V.C.

So whether I was winging it on a sports talk show or becoming a prison culinary master chef or devoting myself to critical programs in an effort to help make the world a better place, I discovered that, despite being planted in the concrete of a maximum security prison, I could thrive. It was all about attitude and perseverance. Sometimes, we can't change our surroundings, but we can always adjust our perspective. As Colossians 3:23-24 (NKJV) says, "And whatever you do, do it heartily, as to the Lord and not to men, knowing that from the Lord you will receive the reward of the inheritance; for you serve the Lord Christ." Even if no one on earth ever acknowledged what I did, I knew God saw. Knowing that I did it for Him gave me satisfaction I had never known before going to prison. That was a good thing since, as far as I knew, I was never going to see the streets again.

CHAPTER 10
THE SEED

"I slept and dreamt life was joy. I awoke and saw life was service. I acted and behold, service was joy." ~Rabindrahath Tagore

From the moment I set foot in Potosi Correctional Center, I resigned myself to the fact that I would never see the streets again. Some men, even those with life sentences or on death row, live with one eye focused on the door, hoping that somehow they would be released. For lifers, that can be detrimental because it leads to so much disappointment. All they can think about is what they are missing outside the prison walls. I decided to accept my fate, try to leave the outside in the past, and focus on creating a full life—as full as is possible in prison—my new "home." That doesn't mean I did not think about home or that I never missed my family. Sure I did! But I was determined to move forward. If you have no hope of physical freedom, it is so much easier to be happy.

I threw myself into every program and activity imaginable. There was one program, however, that would end up being a game-changer, a way-maker, and a calling. Of course, I had no idea about any of that at the time.

My work in the chapel was a lot of fun, and the relationships I formed with other brothers were invaluable. Two such guys were David and Mickey. They were not only chapel workers but also worked for a ministry called Set Free, a Bible study correspondence ministry. They graded courses that inmates in other prisons took. The courses were free for inmates and their families to take, so I got started.

The courses were published by Emmaus Worldwide's Correspondence School in Dubuque, Iowa, a ministry that reaches over 300,000 prisoners in the US every year. A brother on the outside named Randy helped start Set Free Ministries (which distributes Emmaus courses) in 1974 with four other men. Shortly after the ministry began, Randy felt a burden to reach men and women who were incarcerated with the gospel through the Emmaus courses. He would come inside the prison and lead a Bible study once a week. He came up with the idea of using men who were incarcerated and who had already taken the Emmaus courses to grade the courses. That had never been done before, and took a lot of prayer and work, but the Lord made a way for it to happen. David and Mickey were the first two inmate workers for Set Free Ministries. I got to know both of them well, and they, too, like Jay, were amazing brothers in Christ. David and Mickey both had undesirable backgrounds but were new creations in Christ Jesus.[1]

I started taking the Bible courses after I first got to prison because I understood the importance of studying the Bible. But I got so caught up in the recreational activities (basketball, weightlifting, etc.) that I stopped for a while. A few months passed, and I started taking them again. After the third time that I started, it finally stuck. I felt guilty that I spent more time doing other things and not spending time in God's Word like I should. I began sinking my teeth into God's Word, and was able to understand it like never before. My relationship with God began to grow rapidly. Every time I completed a course, I received a certificate. That was great because it gave me, as well as other men, a sense of accomplishment. After completing about thirty courses, I decided to volunteer and work for Set Free. Randy agreed to let me help. I went through the necessary training, and began helping others to grow in their relationship with the Lord.

During that time, I was brought back to court for another crime (previously charged) and was sentenced to two more life sentences, bringing my total to three. It didn't really bother me at all because I had become content with the fact that I was never getting out, and that no matter where I was, I would serve the Lord. Life went on and things didn't change much. Other men came to prison, and a number of us invited them to church and tried to help them get enrolled in the Emmaus courses.

After some time, David and Mickey were both transferred to different prisons. Once again, I lost brothers who had a huge impact in my life. Yet, there were also new brothers in the Lord who came in from the other prisons and jails. The brotherhood that we shared was amazing. Of course, we had our ups and downs, but we remained faithful to God first, and then to one another.

I grew up an only child, so this was a whole new experience for me. I had always wanted a brother or two. The Lord blessed me with many, which was another way that He gave me my heart's desire. We prayed for each other, bore one another's burdens, played games, went to church, cooked meals, did Bible study, and so much more.

God is so good—all the time. He has a way of providing support through new people when circumstances remove others. David and Mickey were gone, but soon Kyle and Don came. Kyle was a brother who was just getting to prison, and quickly got involved in Set Free. Don was a brother who had been in prison before, and had been convicted of murder and sentenced to death row. Don began taking Emmaus courses in the county jail, and gave his life to Christ. Both he and Kyle would take over where David and Mickey left off.

A couple of us also went out to the prison yard and invited other men who were of other religions—or who didn't believe in God—to church. That was always an adventure. Everything one can imagine took place at some time or another. From almost fighting and getting our lives threatened to people coming to Christ and becoming solid brothers, we saw it all. I felt badly because I had basically cut off my outside family, but I was loving my new family in Christ.

Over time, Randy's Bible study got too big, and a few of us suggested that we have a few mini-Bible studies during the same time his was going on. Guys embrace religion in prison for many reasons. Christianity was usually at the bottom of the list, if on the list at all. Christianity was seen as being a weak religion and that it was for the white man. The ones who gave Christ a try saw that He was real and that Christianity was anything but weak, but that didn't keep most people who accept Christ in prison from being picked on and disrespected.

Having mini-Bible studies led by inmates helped in several ways. First of all, not everyone was at the same level of understanding, so many people wouldn't even understand what Randy was teaching. Secondly, many of the men were coming as a result of some of us inviting them, and they only felt comfortable around us. We decided that there would be an intermediate group that Kyle would lead, and a beginner group that Walter and I would lead. The idea was to give the guys a chance to work their way up in difficulty of teaching so that they could really grasp the basics, and be in a setting conducive to asking questions they may have. As they grew in their walk and understanding, they could move on to the next Bible study if they wanted.

That was my first experience with teaching others about the Word of God in a group setting. That was a huge blessing in my life because it motivated me to get into the Word of God more. Knowing that I was helping to impact other's lives gave me a different sense of godly responsibility. It was during that time that I began to really mature in Christ.

The other brothers and I didn't stop at just wanting to lead Bible studies, though. Several of us got together with the chaplain and asked if we could start some sort of Christian council that would help with everything related to our church. We received the okay. Then we began meeting, thinking things through, and figuring out how to make the most of our church activities.

For example, Prison Fellowship came four times a year to do seminars. The director for Missouri was great, and so were most of the volunteers. However, the curriculum was old and not really effective. We met with the director, and shared our thoughts and concerns with her. We got the green light to restructure almost everything. We stuck to the same format, but used different material and took a different approach to trying to reach everyone at the seminar. It was a success! God truly honored our efforts and enthusiasm. The seminar grew from around twenty people attending a weekend to around seventy!

We implemented all sorts of fun and exciting ways to learn about Christ. In time, we actually had Islamic leaders attend our seminars regularly. The inmates enjoyed our new ways of presenting the gospel. We would write plays to act out the Bible. We converted some popular TV game shows to Christ-centered game shows and had Scripture memory contests with prizes. All of that may not sound like much, but it was huge in prison. As Christians, we should understand that anytime a nonbeliever is exposed to the Truth, then it's a success because a seed has been planted.

That was what life looked like for me for the next several years. My life was one giant routine. I worked a job, which by then was in the recreation department. I volunteered for Set Free, led Bible studies, mentored people, helped plan Prison Fellowship Seminars, and played any and every sport that was going on at the time. I had a busy life, and I was happy.

While I was planting the seeds of the gospel into the lives of those around me and even in other prisons through my work with Set Free, God was planting seeds of His own for my benefit. I was just living my life, content to be serving the Lord behind bars. But God was using this service, not just for His kingdom in there, but to show a steady faithful pattern over many years that I was indeed a life changed. He was instilling within my heart a passion for Him, for others, and for life beyond the here and now. He was also beginning to plant the idea into others that perhaps I was meant for more than a prison cell.

We can never know what God has planned. He usually doesn't choose to give us a heads-up on His bigger picture. He wants to see if we will be faithful with whatever He calls us to do, even if we do not see any earthly gain for ourselves. The things we may see as routine, ordinary, and even mundane may be the testing task to see our heart because He has ideas for things beyond our wildest dreams. Miracles, my friends, may catch us by surprise, but they are masterfully crafted by a God who does nothing impulsively. Faithfulness is always the catalyst to bigger missions for the Kingdom.

But back then, I had no idea that I was even being considered, nor did I have a clue about another blessing being sent my way. One day, I was in my cell grading courses when the mail came around. I received a mysterious letter. I opened it, and it was from a woman named Julie who knew a friend of mine, and he had asked her to write me. Sometimes the best things find us when we aren't even looking for them, but more on that later.

CHAPTER 11

THE INVISIBLE POWER OF PREY

"When you are God's person doing God's will, you are immortal until God is finished with you." ~Dr. David Jeremiah

"I will both lie down in peace, and sleep; for You alone, O Lord, make me dwell in safety." Psalm 4:8 (NKJV)

While I enjoy highlighting the positive side of prison life when one is serving the Lord, prison is still just that—prison. And prison is at its core one of the darkest places on earth. Everyone has seen the TV shows depicting life behind bars. Some shows even profile actual prisons, showing "raw" footage that exposes the carnality and viciousness that characterizes humans when they feel they have nothing left to lose. There is also the misconception that life behind bars is cushy, and that thanks to taxpayer dollars criminals are afforded a life of luxury with all their needs met and paid for—the country club experience as some put it.

If prison is a country club, I have no desire to ever join one on the outside. I seriously doubt country clubs include strip/cavity searches every time a loved one visits—both going and coming from the visit. I doubt the club restaurant offers food that's often expired or food with so little flavor you actually are not sure what you are eating. I doubt the showers are "shower at your own risk," with men who are so enslaved to their sexual frustration that they are willing to do anything to relieve it. I also highly doubt country clubs include a lack of adequate heat in the winter and lack of air conditioning in the summer. No, prison is definitely not a vacation or a spa. It is a gauntlet of social, physical, and mental challenges that, until you experience it for yourself, is hard even to truly imagine.

I met a guy named Charles in the county jail at church. I was nineteen, and he was sixteen. He was awaiting trial for murder. We became pretty good friends while there. I was convicted and sentenced before Charles, so I went off to prison first. I was there several months when I heard that he was convicted and was on his way to where I was. I had kind of learned my way around the prison, such as where not to go and who not to associate with. I had learned when the church services and Bible studies were, and some other important things that would "keep you safe."

I saw Charles after he had been there a few days. I went up to him to give him a handshake and hug, and he was very reluctant to embrace me. I called him by his name, and he told me not to call him that, and gave me a nickname to call him. That really took me by surprise. It didn't seem like the person I knew from the county jail. I had heard that people change when they get to prison, but this was my first experience with that. I still told him where the chapel was and when church services were. He didn't seem interested at all. We parted ways, and I was hurt because that wasn't the Christian brother I knew from before.

Later that day, my cellmate told me that he wanted to talk to me about something. We sat down, and he explained that Charles had decided to "hook up" with one of the most dangerous guys in the prison who was on death row for killing an inmate. I was shocked! He went on to explain that now Charles belonged to that guy. He didn't go into detail about the relationship, but he suggested that I leave my friend alone forever. That was so tough to hear. Charles was a guy

I had a tremendous amount of love for, and I couldn't just abandon my brother. I didn't take my cellmate's advice. I decided that I would continue to treat him as a brother. In time, I was able to persuade him to go to church and participate in our church functions and activities. I avoided talking to Charles about his "friend." We both knew what was up, and I just didn't go there. I got a lot of flak from brothers because I was associating with him. I knew he was really afraid, and that he only made the decision to be with this guy because he felt it was the only way he could survive.

The years went by, and we continued to be as cool with each other as we could. One day after church, a friend approached me and gave me some terrible news. He told me that a group of guys had run into Charles' cell and gang-raped him. I couldn't believe it. It was like a punch to the gut. I later found out that Charles' "friend" was in segregation (prison inside of prison) and wasn't coming out for a while, and that was why those guys violated him. Those types of incidents occur frequently, and one becomes insensitive to them, but this time it was different. It was a friend, and it really hurt to know that this happened to him. He didn't deserve it. No one deserved it. Charles was taken away to segregation along with the other guys who raped him. Charles was granted an appeal on his case and went back to court.

Many months went by. I was on my way to dinner and saw Charles. We looked at each other, and there was an uneasy tension. What would I say? How would I embrace him? What would he say? I went up to him, gave him a hug and asked him how he had been. He said he was fine and proceeded to tell me about his appeal and that he had been reconvicted.

During the time Charles was gone, his friend was let out of segregation. The guys who had raped Charles were all transferred. After seeing Charles and knowing all that had happened to him since he got to prison, I decided to finally talk to him about his relationship with his friend, and tell him that I would stand up with him against the guy.

After a few days, I invited Charles into my cell to have "the talk" with him. I said, "Hey, listen. I've been thinking, and I have decided that I will go with you to have a conversation with your friend to tell him that you don't belong to him anymore—that you belong to Christ. I will stand with you, and no matter what happens, I will have your back."

Now that wasn't an easy thing for me to do. It could potentially cost me my life. I was just so frustrated with what happened to Charles, and I wanted him to experience true freedom in Christ.

He said, "I'll think about it, Louis. I'll get back to ya, but thanks, man."

Several days went by, and I hadn't seen Charles. One evening I was watching TV in my cell when my door opened unexpectedly, and a guy came in. It was Charles' friend. He sat down and told me that we needed to talk. Over the years, I had gotten to know this guy. We were actually spades partners here and there. We knew what each other stood for. He looked me square in the eyes and said, "I should kill you for getting into my business."

Needless to say, I was nervous and ready to defend myself as he continued, "I'm not going to because I know how you feel about Charles. It does speak a lot to your character that you have Charles' back and are willing to risk your life for him. I respect that. I respect the fact that you are trying to live for God and do the right thing." He stood to leave and looked back to say, "But if you ever get into my business again, I will have no problem killing you." With that, he left.

Man, I couldn't believe what had just happened. I was so angry. Charles had gone back and told this guy about our conversation, despite the fact that him doing that could cost me my life. I had been willing to risk mine for him, and instead of taking the help offered, he put a huge target on my back for nothing. He could've declined my offer and just kept it between us. There had been no reason to tell. I had never been betrayed like that before. For a moment, I hated Charles. I wanted to hurt him. That forever changed our relationship. From that day forward, we had a superficial relationship.

I always got the sense that he was sorry for what happened, but he never apologized. I understood that he was trapped in sin and living in fear. His judgment was clouded, and he was incapable of breaking Satan's grip on his life. Charles had life without the possibility of parole, which meant that he was never getting out. His friend was executed some years ago. I still pray that Charles will overcome his fear, turn back to the Lord, lean on Him for protection, and choose to serve Him. Only time will tell.

I am not one who believes in "karma," so to speak. But the idea of "what goes around comes around" is, in some ways, a universal idea. In Christianity, it is stated more like this in Galatians 6:7 (NKJV): "Do not be deceived, God is not mocked; for whatever a man sows, that he will also reap."

I had put my life on the line for a brother. While it almost had dire consequences and had been spurned by the very person that I had been willing to sacrifice myself for, nonetheless it had counted to God. In time, it was my own life that needed defending, and God chose to protect me in the most unlikely of ways.

While in prison, one learns about the people around him (if you're smart). Everyone has a past, some more violent than others. The violent ones are the ones you pay close attention to! There were inmates who had murdered other inmates and even guards inside the prison. I witnessed people trying to take others' lives on many occasions. I had come to know many, if not all, the people who had done these things, and always proceeded with extreme caution when it came to dealing with them.

One person in particular was Carlos G. I had heard from inmates and staff that this was a dangerous guy. He had stabbed many inmates and guards, trying to take their lives. He wasn't a very big guy but, man, you could sense the evil in him.

I was a known Christian in prison, and there were many people who didn't like or respect me or Christianity. In fact, many people hated

Christians. Carlos G. was one of those people. I was particularly hated because I came to prison young, and I chose Christ. I stood on it after being challenged many times. People wanted to hurt me or scare me into renouncing my faith. That was something I faced every day. Behind any corner could be someone waiting for me. Because I put my faith in Christ that He would protect me, I went anywhere I wanted to in the prison and did whatever I wanted to do—not to show off, but to live my life according to how Christ wanted me to. I was deeply hated for that and was told so many times. That was the climate.

I guess Carlos G. wanted to finally do something to me to show everyone that I could be touched, and that my God couldn't protect me. I was sitting on the bleachers with a bunch of others in the gym one day, watching guys play basketball. Suddenly, I saw Carlos G. coming toward the bleachers, so I was on high alert. Something was about to go down with someone. I was at the top, and he continued to pass everyone and sat right in front of me. To make matters worse, he sat down facing me and stared me down. I never looked at him. I just kept watching the game, but I made sure that I could see him in my peripheral vision. After what felt like an hour, he said, "You're lucky, you know that?"

I looked at him and said, "Yes."

I had no idea what he was talking about, but I didn't think asking him what he was talking about or arguing with him would be a good idea.

He said again, "I said, 'You know you're lucky, right?'"

That time, I nodded my head in agreement and said, "Yes, I am."

He continued to stare at me as the tension grew. Then he just left. I had been praying the entire time that if he made a move on me, I wouldn't be out of line defending myself. I admit I was afraid but had stared down the barrel of a gun several times before and wasn't afraid to fight that guy. I wanted to honor God in every situation, but if fighting to defend myself had to happen, I was cool with that. In a strange, crazy way, I kind of hoped he did make a move so that I could try to break his neck for all the crazy things he did to innocent people. I knew that heaven was my home. If I died, I would be with Jesus. Well, after all that, I was still curious about what that guy meant.

Days, weeks, months, and even a few years went by, and I still didn't know. Of course, I wasn't going around asking people; I didn't want to stir the pot. Finally one day, a good friend of mine sat down with me, and we started talking. He was a devout Muslim. We just kicked back and were talking about whatever. After we stopped talking for a few minutes, he said, "You don't know, do you? You really don't know."

I agreed and said, "Yes, I don't know. What the heck are you talking about?"

He told me that a couple of years back a guy (Carlos G.) wanted to take me out. He hated how no one bothered me, I just minded my business, and so many people liked me. He spoke to his Islamic brothers (a different Islamic sect than mainstream Muslims), and they gave him the green light to get me. However, the mainstream Muslims heard about it and told the other sect that if they touched one hair on my head, they would slay all of them. Those were the exact words he told me they used. The Muslims outnumbered that sect by about nine to one! The sect stood down, and that was why Carlos G. told me I was lucky. I just started tearing up and thanking God. Incredible!

To this day, I still can't believe it. The God of the universe chose to use my enemies and His enemies to protect me. Wow. Words cannot express how my relationship and faithfulness to God grew. For years, I had been witnessing to my Muslim friend. It was an amazing way to show him that Jesus and the Bible were real. He admitted to me that he was too involved to change his faith and that he would just have to deal with whatever God does with him. It saddened me that people can see God, know He is real, and still not follow Him. But it didn't take away from the extraordinary way that God wove all of our lives together, and how God could use anyone for His purposes. God saved my life through my friend who may not want my particular faith but who could see it for what it was.

As I said, prison is a dark, often evil place. But light still shines there. I am human. I admittedly was often nervous or afraid or uncertain. If God had chosen to not protect my earthly life and had called me home by way of either Charles's friend or Carlos G., He still would've been just as good and just as sovereign. However, my work for Him wasn't done yet, so I was invincible as long as I followed His lead. The same is true for anyone.

CHAPTER 12
BIG D

"God has put something noble and good into every heart His hand created." ~Mark Twain

One of the hardest aspects of prison was that when I had an issue with someone, I just couldn't get away from him. While I always tried to honor God in my life, my attitude, and my actions, I am still human. I do not enjoy taking guff from others. At all. On the streets, if I was annoyed or angry, I could leave a situation or get even. But in prison, there was nowhere to go. I was literally boxed in, which did have its advantages. When I found myself hating the situation or wondering how on earth to change it, I fell to my knees in prayer.

God has a unique sense of problem-solving. Sometimes, His solutions made me push back rather than surrender. But God is persistent, and like Jonah with Nineveh, God's will always gets accomplished. It was just up to me how quickly I was going to get on board with cooperating. When I finally did, God's way definitely ended up teaching me as many lessons as He did the other guy.

Every Tuesday and Thursday, people transferred in and out. That included people who had been newly convicted, as well as people coming from other prisons. Sometimes, they were transferred for disciplinary reasons or because they were at a particular prison for a long time. (Prison administration called this "staff familiarity" and felt that the inmate and some staff might establish a relationship which could lead to escape or other rules being broken.)

I was in the gym one day, and I saw a guy I had never seen before. The reason he was so noticeable was because he was "mean mugging" me. ("Mean mugging" is staring at someone with a mean look.) I just turned my head and continued with what I was doing.

I quickly learned that this guy had already been locked up about twenty years and had even done time before that current conviction. He was old school and definitely institutionalized. I wasn't really tripping because at that point I had already been locked up over ten years myself. I knew how to carry myself and definitely knew how to deal with people like that. I didn't think too much about it until I found this guy in my face, mean mugging me and asking me who I was. I told him my name and asked him who he was. He said that if I didn't know then I better find out. He turned and walked away. Man! Now, I had to deal with another idiot.

Why, God? I thought. *Haven't I been through enough of these battles?*

Every day from that point on, this guy tried to make my life a living hell. I found that I wasn't the only one. He was targeting everyone who proclaimed Christ as their King. The picture that came to mind was that we were a flock of sheep, and he was a wolf stalking us. It was weird because we all saw him bothering each of us individually, but we never went to one another to talk about it. I didn't really feel that intimidated by him, which made it worse. He wanted to break me, and I was trying to not be broken while keeping a Christlike manner. This was the toughest situation I had faced because it was a *continuous* attack. It got so bad that I had friends who were nonbelievers asking me if I needed help. They couldn't stand this guy either and would have loved to bust his head. He never bothered them because he knew it would be ON. I told them to leave him alone—that God would take care of the situation.

Although these friends were nonbelievers, they knew Who I served, and I used every opportunity to witness to them. They were mostly into Islam, just like the guy who kept bothering me. However, he was in a different group than them. Just as in Christianity, I learned that Islam has different "denominations" or "sects," and they could be different in their behaviors. In time, the verbal confrontations turned into physical ones. He would bump into me, and push me around. It took everything I had not to wring his neck. I prayed like crazy throughout this whole ordeal and got nothing from God. All I could do was remain faithful to His Word and continue to turn the other cheek.

One night, I was awakened from my sleep, and all I could think about was taking this guy on a food visit with me. (A "food visit" was like a regular visit, but your family could bring you home-cooked or fast food. You had to have good conduct and have not gotten into trouble to be eligible to go.) I was so mad. I just knew that God wasn't telling me to take this guy on a food visit with me. I couldn't get back to sleep; I just kept telling God that this WASN'T going to happen. I mean, what would everyone think? I knew what they would think. They would think that he finally broke me, and that he was taking advantage of me. I couldn't live with everyone thinking that. After I wrestled with it for a while, it started to seem more and more like an okay idea. Just okay. I decided to go with it, and prayed. I told God that this had to be from Him and that I was going through with it. I told God that if I got into a fight and hurt him, it was going to be on God.

Praying was the easy part. The next step was to go to him and invite him on the visit. For the first time, I approached him. He gave me the craziest look I had ever seen. He cocked his head, put his hands on his hips, and looked at me as if to say, "You have the audacity to approach *me*?" I confidently asked him if he wanted to go on the food visit with me. He continued to look crazy and then just walked away. I thought, *That didn't go too badly.*

Later that day, he asked me, "What did you say earlier?"

He had heard me; I was quite clear. I think he was in disbelief. I proceeded to tell him, "Listen, God put it on my heart to invite you to my food visit."

He shook his head and told me, "You better not be playin' with me."

"Trust me. I definitely wouldn't be playing with you."

"I need to think about it."

"Okay, but I'll need an answer soon so that we can put in for the approval."

He came back to me a few days later, and said that he would go with me.

I said, "Cool. What would you like to eat?"

He answered, "It doesn't matter. I've never been on a visit since I've been incarcerated. Anything will be fine."

My heart sank. This guy had been locked up over twenty years and NEVER had a visit. No one cared about this guy. That shouldn't be so. So I told him, "I want you to have whatever your favorite meal is. If it is something my mother can't make, then she will go buy it."

"I don't know, man."

"My mom is good at making lasagna. She's Italian. We will have that with all the trimmings. She can bring dessert too."

"Cheesecake?"

I smiled. "Sure, cheesecake. A big one with cherries on it."

He got the biggest smile on his face just talking about it. I started to view this guy in a different light. I began to see that this guy wasn't that mean after all. I learned that he had come to prison in his early teens and that he had a really rough time. How he acted was the only way he knew how to act. Our relationship would never be the same.

We got all of the paperwork filled out and submitted, and then we waited for approval. That was the part that I worried about. I didn't worry that the approval wouldn't go through, but that this was where everyone would see that he was going on a visit with me. Sure enough, it started.

Friends and even brothers in Christ questioned my decision. Some were even upset that I had invited this "heathen" over them. I could see their point, but I told them that God told me to do this.

While we were waiting for the big day, he came to me and had questions. Who was coming? How should he address them? Could he be part of the conversation? I told him that while he was there he could be part of our family and that he could just be himself. I knew that might be dangerous to tell him that, but that's what came out. I gave my family the heads-up on him so they would know what to expect.

The day came, and we went into the visiting room. I introduced him to everyone, and we sat down. That day, my mom, my aunt, and my stepfather came to see me. I could hardly get him to eat anything. He was so nervous and trying to be polite. Mom had brought lasagna, garlic cheese bread, salad, and cherry cheesecake. I just kept piling food onto his plate; that forced him to eat. We had a good time. My family showed him love, and I can truly say that it blessed my heart. When we left, everyone gave him hugs. I never knew he could smile so much. He later told me that taking him on that visit was the nicest thing anyone had ever done for him!

I don't know about the rest of his life, but that day he experienced the love of family and, more importantly, the love of God. From that day on, we became cordial. No, we didn't become best friends. No, he didn't accept Christ. He said he couldn't lose his reputation because he thought that it would make him weak and people wouldn't respect him. I tried to help him see that it would show people how strong he really was. I did get him to ease up on bothering my Christian brothers, though.

I learned so much through that experience. I began to see exactly why God tells us to love our enemies, to bless those that curse us, to do good to those who hate us, and to pray for those who spitefully use and persecute us.[1] It is so easy to be generous to those we like. But that does not give us a full picture of Christ who sacrificed Himself on the cross for everyone, despite the fact that each of us started by hating

Him and rejecting Him. He died knowing that so many would choose to reject Him and never accept Him (like Big D), but He did it anyway. He didn't do it because *we* are good. He did it because *He* is good.

The experience with Big D drew me closer to Christ and allowed me to have a deeper relationship with God—a depth of intimacy that only comes with obeying Him, even when the command He gives is the exact opposite of what we want to do. I certainly didn't sacrifice my life for the guy the way Christ did for us, but somehow I got a better understanding for Christ's submission to the Father to die on the cross, and how God was well pleased with His Son. Whether or not Big D ever became a Christian didn't really affect the outcome. I am not responsible for his choice. I was only responsible for my obedience. Admittedly, I didn't obey immediately and even questioned God's request. But I am so thankful that eventually I did what God wanted. Maybe Big D was blessed by it, but I was blessed even more.

CHAPTER 13
JULIE

"Courage is saying 'yes' to life even when our heart is pounding."
~Dr. Steve Leary

Being in prison as a lifer meant that I had long since resigned myself to the reality that a wife and family would never happen. Sure, some guys in prison for life, or even on death row, get married while they are behind bars, but that is not the norm. That was especially unusual for a prison like Potosi which didn't even allow conjugal visits. I did know a few guys who met and married while behind bars despite knowing they would never see the streets again. Don was one such guy. He met a journalist who became interested in the unique circumstances of his case. In the course of her investigating things, they fell in love. Truly. Sincerely. They married and developed a love story that would end tragically when he was executed, despite her tireless efforts to get the death sentence repealed. But they loved each other to the end.

However, for most people, the separation is just too hard. Unless a guy came into camp (prison) married, he usually remained single. That had been my plan, as well. I just couldn't see the benefit, either to myself or to a woman, to deal with everything that would be part of the package of being in a relationship with someone, when we would know that we would never really get to be together. Friendships were fine, but even those I relegated to ones formed with other inmates. I kept in touch with a handful of friends on the streets, but most I had let go of—not because they didn't matter to me but because it was just too hard to constantly be reminded of everything I was missing out there. It felt healthier to just shut the door on that life and make the most of the life I had on the inside. I insulated myself as much as possible from the outside world.

With the exception of my mother and some close friends and family, I managed to build a fairly impenetrable wall around my life. Unlike the prison wall, though, that wall was for my protection, not that of society. Somehow I missed a spot, however, and like so much of my life, God had ideas for me that I never even dreamed of. This time that idea was named Julie.

One random day in September 2003, I was in my cell grading courses when the mail came around. I received a mysterious letter. I opened it, and it was from a woman named Julie who knew my friend Larry. Larry was one of my best friends from the outside. Larry and Julie worked together, and he had asked her if she knew anyone who would want to write to me so that I could get some mail. About a month later, she was laid off and had some extra time on her hands, so she decided to write to me herself. She didn't really know what to say so she encouraged me by telling me that she was sorry to hear about my circumstances and to keep my head up.

I didn't know what to do. This person had penetrated the bubble I had created around myself. I really didn't want anything to do with the outside world because I saw the heartache and pain that people went through trying to live in prison and on the street. Yet, I decided to write back and at least thank her for the kind words, and to tell her that it was only by the grace of God that I had made it this far. I told her that through Him, I would continue to make it. She wrote back. She sent a letter explaining how she learned about my situation, and we just continued to write back and forth. At first, it was just general things.

She would talk about going grocery shopping or whatever, and I would tell her about what I was up to any given week.

Over the months, it started to shift to something more meaningful. I couldn't figure out why she was writing more or showing me so much love. It went from one letter a week to literally four to five letters a day, five days a week by both of us. About a month into it, she gave me my friend's phone number and told me that she would be with him that weekend if I wanted to call and talk to her. I called her, but she was on her way to a movie, so we didn't talk long. I tried to have my friend do a three-way call, but the night I called her, they were at a party or somewhere noisy. Julie barely talked. I was so upset that I went back to my cell and told my cellmate that I wouldn't be calling her again because she barely talked. I figured she wasn't really that interested. But I found out that she just couldn't hear very well because of all the noise. She made it clear that she was still interested in talking when she gave me her direct number.

In January, Julie decided to visit me. She was from Chicago, so for her to come visit in person meant a six-hour drive. I arranged for her to come to all of the visiting sessions, including a few hours in the Friday night session. There were two visiting sessions a day (morning and afternoon) both Saturday and Sunday, as well as a 4:00-8:00 block Tuesday through Friday. At the last minute, however, she told me that she had to cancel because she had to work—or so she said.

I was disappointed, but I figured we'd make it happen another time. So Friday afternoon I went to play basketball instead. Afterward, I took a shower. Just as I got back to my cell, I got a call that I had a visitor. Since I hadn't been expecting anyone, my hair was all out and big. The guard told me that I had a hot chick waiting for me. I didn't believe him and instead worried that it was bad news.

When I finally got to the visiting room, I saw a woman sitting by the guard's desk. I had a few pictures of Julie, and I recognized her right away. It turned out that Julie didn't have to work; she just wanted to surprise me. I started walking toward her, but a little girl was at the table getting a game. She stepped on my flip flop and pulled it off. It was such a small thing, but it set into motion an awkward first meeting. Julie didn't get up to give me a hug, and I was too nervous to ask her if I could give her one. I saw a sergeant who I was cool with and asked him if he could make sure that Julie was on the visitor's list for the entire weekend. Since I thought she had to cancel, I hadn't requested her to be on the list. The sergeant was nice enough to go out in the pouring rain, back to the housing unit to check. He came back an hour or so later and said that he would take care of it so that Julie could visit. We were so thankful that Julie hadn't driven all that way for just a few hours on Friday. God just kept looking out for us.

After her first visit, Julie visited about every six weeks for the first couple of years. On the first visit, we didn't buy any picture cards (photos that were available at visits), but after that we bought ones for each visit. Julie went back to the hotel and changed clothes between each session to help it feel like we were getting to do more dates. It was an unconventional arrangement, but we both did everything we could to make it feel normal. In some ways, the distance and restrictions allowed us to truly get to know each other on a deeper level. As we wrote letters, talked on the phone, and saw each other face-to-face during her visits, I saw how genuine, gentle, and soft-spoken she was. I may not have been looking to meet someone, and maybe I was even worried to let myself get attached, but for some reason I just needed to keep talking to her.

Eventually I surprised her by inviting my mom and stepdad, too, so that they could all meet in person. It just felt like the logical thing to do. I wanted her to know she was special in my life. There was so much that I couldn't control. I knew it worried her when she expected a call from me, but something would happen in the prison which caused all of us to be locked down. It was not protocol to alert families or put a message online so that loved ones would know why they didn't hear from us. Instead, she would have to wait until she heard from me at some later time to know if everything was okay. In fact, to call the prison and ask if a specific inmate was okay could potentially get that inmate unwanted attention—questions into what's going on that had family calling. So the only thing to do was wait.

But what I could control was letting her know she mattered. Surprising her with meeting my parents was just one of the things I tried to do to let her know. For me, something was different. Julie didn't feel like a coincidence; it felt like she was placed in my life for a reason. I just wasn't sure how far that reason went yet. We were two different people from two different walks of life. That made for some great conversations. As we continued getting to know each other, we decided that we wanted to see what life would be like as a couple. I had no idea if I was ever going to get out of prison, and I made that clear to her. I made sure that I was honest and upfront with her. In the beginning, it was quite easy to be honest because I had no interest for a relationship. In fact, for the first few months it was all about my case and what happened and the fact that I was never getting out of prison. Well, almost never getting out...

CHAPTER 14
NEWS OF A LIFETIME

"Everything comes to him who hustles while he waits."
~Thomas A. Edison
"But Jesus looked at them and said, 'With men it is impossible, but
not with God; for with God all things are possible.'"
~Mark 10:27 (NKJV)

They say a watched pot never boils. They say that the best things come when you're not looking for them. I think that is partially true. It certainly seemed to be true in meeting Julie. I was never one of those inmates who lived counting the days until my release, largely because as far as I knew, if I did get released, I would be a very old man. However, just because the chances were slim didn't mean that I didn't still want to be the best I could be, whether inside or outside of those concrete walls. So I busied myself with everything, including getting to know Julie better. We met in 2003, and we knew I had a parole board hearing in 2007, but neither of us held out much hope that it would bring good news.

Here's how Missouri's sentencing and parole system works—or at least how it worked at the time. Even though I had multiple life sentences plus 100 years, I technically still had a chance of being released. In Missouri, the parole board has all the power to do what they want. I knew of a few people who had one life sentence, and they did twenty to twenty-five years before the board released them. I had two lives and 100 years, which meant that if they made me do twenty years on each life, that would be forty years. In the Missouri Probation and Parole handbook, any sentence over thirty years is to be considered a life sentence. That meant that I would have to do another twenty years for that. So all together I would have to serve 60 years before I would be released. Since I was twenty when I got started, I would be roughly eighty years old when I would get out. So in my mind, I wasn't getting out. The way I saw it, my parole board meeting in 2007 was a mere formality. Of course, my life was in God's hands.

If I had one wish, it would have been that I would only have to do twenty years, and the parole board would give me a chance. The time came, and I went for my hearing. The parole room was in the hallway on the way to the visiting room. I was allowed to bring one person with me. I chose my mother because she had been with me the entire journey. We walked into the room. The parole board was behind a table with two chairs facing them. We sat down. We were in with them about ten minutes. It went nothing like I thought or heard it would. I had been told by other people that they would ask all kinds of crazy questions to try to push my buttons. The exact opposite happened. The board said that it seemed like I was a good person and that I had just gotten mixed up with the wrong crowd. They said that they didn't believe I would make the same mistakes again. I couldn't believe what I was hearing. I was basically a bobblehead, agreeing with everything they said.

I left, and it hit me: they had no intention of letting me out, so they just wanted to get to the next person on the list. Why ask the tough stuff if they weren't considering letting me go?

I went back to my housing unit to report to everyone how things went. Most people don't know this, but seeing the parole board is a pretty big deal, especially when most of the people in the prison are never getting out. In some instances, people who will never get out will kind of cheer for some who have a chance. I was told I would hear an answer in four to six weeks. After a few days, I forgot about it.

One day while waiting to go to a Set Free training session with Randy and the other workers, my name, along with many others, was called to go to the caseworker's office. I'll never forget when I heard the guy yell out, "It's the answers from the parole board!"

I just thought, *Okay, cool.* I was the first one through the door. I sat and waited as they called everyone else before me except for one person. The only reason he had not gone was because he was still at work in the kitchen. The kitchen didn't play. It didn't matter what was going on; they weren't letting anybody leave early until the work was done. A caseworker came out of her office and asked me what was going on. I told her that I was waiting on an answer from the parole board. I was really frustrated and said it loudly so the guy reading the answers could hear me.

He looked up over the top of his reading glasses and called my name.

I jumped up and said, "Yes, sir."

The man waved me over. "Have a seat."

I sat down, and he proceeded to read from a piece of paper that stated I was scheduled for release February 10, 2009. In that moment, time froze for me. My first thought was that it couldn't be true. I thought that he was reading the other guy's paper. He started to hand me the paper, and I almost snatched it out of his hand. I immediately started rubbing the paper in between my fingers to make sure it was one page and that it was MY page. It was, and what he read was true.

I broke down crying right there, saying, "Thank you, Jesus!"

I went into the lobby and caseworkers from all over the place were trying to see what all the commotion was about. One caseworker took the paper from my hand and read it out loud. People started clapping. One guy came over and gave me a hug and said, "God bless you. I know you are going to make it."

To this day, I do not have an explanation of why I was given a release date. I wasn't and haven't ever been told anything. In some ways, that is often how God is with us. He doesn't choose to tell us the whys of things He allows in our lives or does on our behalf. When it is bad news, that can be a stumbling block because we feel like we need to know. But in this case, as curious as I am, I am okay without knowing the why or the how. All I know is that it was a miracle. God literally opened prison doors for me. I had no idea why, but I knew I had to make it count. I would soon find that being released, while a definite blessing, would lead to challenges I never imagined.

CHAPTER 15
888 DAYS TO FREEDOM

"God always gives His best to those who leave the choice with Him."
~Jim Elliot

Being blindsided by a release date was the best possible type of blindside. It was a miracle beyond my wildest dreams. Nothing prepared me for that. Unlike so many, I had not been spending my years behind bars trying to find loopholes in the legal system to get myself released. Maybe it helped that I didn't really believe it was possible, especially not before I was an old man. Or maybe it was because I had come to the conclusion that I just wanted to serve God with my life, and I could do that in prison as well as I could out of prison. But there I was holding a piece of paper with a miracle written in black ink.

While apostles like Peter and Paul were sometimes released from prison through miraculous means, they had been imprisoned for serving Christ. I had no expectation of being released early from my sentence. But unlike biblical times, I didn't get to just walk out the front door when I received the news of my miracle.

After I was given a two-and-a-half-year release date, I was immediately handcuffed and taken to the hole. Because I was given that date, my security custody level was dropped from a level five to a level two, and I could no longer be around the guys I had done time with in the prior thirteen years. That was a safety thing the state did to protect themselves. The law stated that certain custody levels couldn't be around one another. Because of that, I wasn't able to say goodbye to any of my brothers in Christ or anyone else. I was also unable to use the phone to tell any of my family the great news. Fortunately, I knew a guy who could make phone calls. I gave him my mother's and Julie's numbers to call. He got through to Julie, and he said that she was just screaming on the phone in disbelief. A few days later, she was able to talk to my mother.

I was in the hole for about two weeks, awaiting transfer. I didn't know where I was going until the day they put me on the bus. I got to the new prison and was immediately afraid. I was afraid because I saw inmates walking around with shovels and tool boxes—something that never happened at a level five maximum security prison. I was afraid of getting into it with someone. What if they had a pitch fork or hammer or something? I just wasn't ready for all of that.

I immediately went into protection mode. That meant watch everyone and use the eyes in the back of my head! I was used to that, but never had to worry much about those types of weapons.

I received my new state issue clothing—more gray-and-white—and went to my housing unit. It was just like coming to prison all over again. Algoa was three to four times bigger than Potosi. There were around 700 inmates at Potosi, but there were easily double or triple that at Algoa. The housing units were two level, and the buildings were made out of river rock. They were built in the early 1900s, which meant it was outdated. When I walked into my new housing unit and saw that I was going to be living in a dorm, something I hadn't done since the county jail days, a new fear kicked in. I was so used to being in a cell and not surrounded by people that I didn't think I was going to make it. I went in, found my bunk, and sat down—just like my first day in county jail.

We had metal lockers to put our belongings in, but I didn't have a lock to lock it up. I felt I couldn't leave the dorm because I didn't want anyone to take my stuff. I was tripping! After sitting there a few minutes, I saw a guy who I knew from the prison I just left. I immediately went to him to ask a slew of questions. He told me that all the people locked up here were going home in three years or less. There weren't big problems there like the place I had just left. Sure there were fights and robberies, but not too often because guys didn't want to get a new crime and be sent back to a prison like Potosi. That made sense and gave me some relief. I found out that I would have to stay in the dorm about two weeks, then I'd be placed in a cell. The weeks couldn't go by fast enough. I made it through and felt that as soon as I was in my new cell I'd be able to sleep at night. Sleeping with one eye open had gotten old quickly.

I got moved into the cell only to find out that they didn't lock! Man, another crazy thing! Just when I thought I would get some relief, I found that there was none. Then I thought to myself, *Oh well. I am going home in a few years, and I can make it through this.* I repeated that to myself often.

It wasn't just the lack of security that took some getting used to. Since the building was so old, it did not have central heating or cooling—no heat and no air conditioning. It was either very hot or very cold. The summers were actually harder than the winters. In the summer, I would take a bath towel, drench it with ice water, wear just boxers, put the cold towel on a fan with a clip, and rig my sheet to make a wind tunnel. That provided some temporary relief before having to repeat the process all over again.

While I found adjusting to my new "home" a little more challenging than I had imagined, it didn't take long for me to find my old groove, which meant that instead of watching the calendar slowly tick down, I threw myself into life there and was quickly almost as busy as I had been at Potosi. I ran into several people I knew from the other prison, and we hung out. We compared the differences of the two places and made fun of how the guys in that prison didn't know what doing real time was like.

I managed to get a job in recreation and started getting acquainted with the new surroundings. It wasn't too long before I was officiating sports leagues, thanks to the recreation officers at the place I just left. After about a year, I became the inmate sports commissioner and was running all the sports leagues and creating various tournaments for the guys. That was what I loved to do, and God blessed me with the opportunity to do it.

Of course, just like on the streets, sports proved to be brutal to my body. In 2008, during a routine game of flag football, I fell on the ball and broke two ribs. I began coughing up blood. Going to the emergency room is a pain in regular life. Try doing it shackled in the box—which is the waist chain. I was in so much pain. Because of the nature of my injury, they could not just take care of me at the prison infirmary, so I was transferred to a regular hospital, which I liked. It was a change of scenery. Guards with shotguns were on either side. I had to take off my own shirt and shorts, and wear state issue. I spent one night in the hospital, and while I was there I saw someone from Potosi working at the hospital as an inmate.

I easily survived, healed, and moved on from my flag football injury. Most of my days at Algoa were largely routine and uneventful. There were pros and cons (no pun intended) to being there. The biggest pro was that I was on a countdown to when I'd be going home. Once it got under a hundred days, I started counting. Fear crept in again as the days grew closer. It was a new, different type of fear—the fear of the unknown mixed with elation from being released after fifteen-and-a-half years.

What was I going to do now that I'd be out? Would I find a job, and if so, what would it be? I didn't know how to do much. Would people accept me despite my past? Would people look at me or talk to me and know I'd been in prison? Would I find a good church to become part of? Those were just a few questions going through my mind. I was able to cope with everything, though, because I knew that Christ was the head of my life and that He would direct my steps. I wouldn't have to worry about any of that stuff as long as I remained faithful to Him. After all, it was only because of Him that I was getting released in the first place. He had to have a reason and a plan for making that happen.

For all of the uncertainties, though, two things remained constant in my life: my walk with the Lord and my relationship with Julie. We knew we loved each other, even back when I thought the chances of me seeing the streets before I was an old man seemed slim to none. I even brought up marriage but nothing formal. I had no intention of marrying her while I was in prison. Then I received the out date, and though it got pushed back an additional six months because of a miscalculation, I couldn't help but think it was time. Time to allow myself some real world plans. So I designed a ring and asked my mother to get it made. Julie didn't get to visit often while I was at Algoa because of the additional distance and other factors. But one weekend, she, my mother, and my stepfather all visited on the same day. My mother brought the ring in. Julie and I were already at the table when my parents arrived. I excused myself to go to the vending machine with my mom, and she gave me the ring. I walked back to the table. I asked Julie if she would marry me and put the ring on her finger. It may not have been a Hollywood proposal, but it was real and loving and witnessed by the other person who mattered most to me. Did we need anything more than that?

Before I knew it, 888 days had passed. The night before my release on August 5, 2009, I slept pretty well. I got up early, showered, and dressed. They had me processed and checked out by 7 a.m., but I had to wait another two hours before they opened the doors for my release. I sat patiently, sitting in street clothes for the first time in almost sixteen years. Finally it was 9 a.m., and I was told it was time. I stood up and walked to the door. No chains. No armed escort. The door opened. I walked out. The sun and breeze hit my face uninhibited by wall or fence. I took a step forward. I was free.

PART III
LOVE

CHAPTER 16
OUT OF THE FRYING PAN AND INTO THE FIRE

"Shoot for little victories every day, and with the little victories they will stack up to a good result." ~Ken Tucker

On the day those prison doors opened, it felt like my life was starting over. I had never been on the streets as a Christian. The only life I knew on the outside was one so radically different than the life I had carefully built for myself behind bars. It was not lost on me the gravity of what had led me to that day. Getting released from prison is ultimately any inmate's dream. Now my dream was a reality. I could hug my family. Talk to them whenever I wanted to. I could, in theory, create a brand new life for myself. And for that, I was so grateful. Yet, the fact remained that finally leaving the confines of a prison cell did not mean an automatic happily ever after. In fact, within a few minutes of walking out the door, I got a cold hard dose of reality.

I stepped out of prison and was struck by the wide openness. I felt like running in all directions just because I could. But I didn't. I had more important things to do as I was immediately greeted by my stepfather and Julie. What a sight for sore eyes. That was the first time I was meeting either of them outside of a visiting room, and to hug

Julie without guards watching and for as long as I wanted to—wow. It felt so good.

My mother, however, was not out to greet me. She hadn't been up to visit me in the recent months, either. Julie told me that Mom was in the car. I walked over to the car to see her and was shocked. Even my aunt's phone call trying to warn me that she had changed didn't prepare me. I didn't even recognize her. Her normally curly brown hair was gray and straight. She had lost so much weight that she was no longer full and healthy, but skinny. The cancer I knew that she had clearly had ravaged her body. It was like a punch to the gut. I was finally free—and my mother was dying.

When my mother first found out she had cancer, it wasn't life-threatening, but it did require treatment. She needed two surgeries, and initially she didn't want to have any surgery. I was still in prison at the time, and I threatened to take her off my visiting list and stop calling if she didn't. She agreed to have the surgery and had just completed the first one when we got the news that I was going to be released. She decided to delay the second surgery because she was scared of dying during it and not seeing me get released. That was a fatal decision. It was never something she should die from, but her decision to postpone the second surgery until my release gave the cancer years to spread, and by the time I was released there was nothing they could do. The woman who had been through it all with me, for better or for worse, was going to leave me just as I was finally getting to go home to her.

I smiled at my mom, and we greeted each other. Neither of us talked about the obvious turn of events. We all got in the car and headed out. I couldn't get away fast enough. I knew they weren't going to change their minds and make me go back in, but it didn't matter. I just wanted to get out of there. We stopped at a gas station. That sounds like such a simple thing, but for me, it was almost overwhelming. So many choices! There were candy bars and snacks that weren't even in existence when I was locked up. In the end, I picked out a Pepsi, 100 Grand Bar, and chips.

We talked about going for dinner, but I decided that I just wanted to get home. It had not even been an hour, and I was exhausted emotionally.

We talked about going for dinner, but I decided that I just wanted to get home. It had not even been an hour, and I was exhausted emotionally. We reached my mom's house; almost immediately I fell asleep. Four hours later I woke up hungry as a hostage. Everything suddenly sounded so good. We decided to get Taco Bell and possibly even a pizza to go with it. It had been so long. Funny what you miss when you can't have it. I couldn't really do anything else. I needed to wait for my ankle bracelet and to find out what I could and couldn't do on parole.

Julie still lived in Chicago and had to leave to go back to work. It was hard to say goodbye, but I had a lot of things to sort out before it could even be feasible for me to think about getting married and moving to Chicago—most notably spending time with my mom. And I had to work it out with the parole board. I was under Missouri's parole supervision. For me to move to Chicago meant that I had to get permission from them because it entailed them asking Illinois to monitor me on their behalf as part of the Interstate Compact.

In the meantime, I needed a job. A job. Sounds like such a simple next step. But your prospects are finished the moment you have to check that tiny little box next to "Have you ever committed a felony?" I couldn't find a job. I couldn't have any contact with any of the men I had just spent the last fifteen years with, which made life on the outside feel very isolating at first. Thankfully, Randy didn't just care about people on the inside of prison. While Missouri law said that to be a volunteer you had to either work with inmates on the inside OR work with released inmates (but not both), Randy didn't seem to think that was set in stone. He went to higher-ups within the justice system to get special permission to work with me on the outside while still being a VIC (volunteer in corrections) on the inside. God let him find favor with them, and they said yes. Randy and his son Grant (also a VIC) happened to have a mowing business and hired me on. It was a lot of work, but it was a job, and I was thankful for it. I was also thankful to have contact with at least a few people that I had regularly interacted with while in prison.

In the fifteen years that I was locked up, miraculously almost no one in my family died. Many inmates will tell you that losing a loved one and not being able to attend the funeral is one of the most difficult parts of being incarcerated. The only person who did die while I was in prison was an uncle, and he passed away shortly before my release. I was grateful that God preserved both Grandma Velma and my mother until I was released. Outside of meeting Christ as my Savior, that was the biggest blessing of my life: seeing them as a free man. Grandma Velma died a week after I was released. She was 103 years old.

Amid all of the chaos of life on the outside, I was also trying to move forward in my relationship with Julie. In hindsight, I can't really explain the timing, but we decided to get married despite not being able to live in the same city. On September 18, 2009, Julie and I, along with my aunt, went to the courthouse and were married. Afterward she treated us to lunch at the 54th Street Grill to celebrate. Then Julie had to leave for Chicago again.

Eventually, I received permission from my parole officer to move to Chicago. In November 2009, I moved, and for the first time got to really start a life with Julie. Challenges followed me. Finding a job proved difficult. I no longer had any connections like I did with Randy. For months, I tried without any success to find something—anything—to call employment. As I tried in vain to find a job, I had another crushing blow. On December 26, 2009—just months after my release—my mother passed away. The grief that washed over me was indescribable.

While winter was a time of grief for me that year, spring came and with it came a chance at a job. I found a class that helped inmates fill out applications, etc. They had me do an online test, and from that I was offered a job selling rooftop tickets to Cubs games. Basically, it was calling thousands of businesses via cold calls and attempting to get them to buy a group outing. It was 100 percent commission, but they gave a stipend of $2,000. What I did not realize at first, however, was that if I didn't sell enough to cover the $2,000, I had to pay it back! I was trying to sell all-inclusive tickets for a rooftop venue across from the field for $150 per person.

I didn't manage to sell anything the first month. I had no idea how to just randomly call businesses asking them to dish out potentially thousands of dollars for a work event. It didn't even feel like the best economy to be trying, but I stuck at it and slowly learned how to approach it effectively. By the time the season was over, I had been given about $8,000 in stipend but only made between $1,500-$2,000 in sales. I was so worried they were going to make me pay them back. But God is good, and they did not make me pay them back, and even gave me a $100 gift card to Olive Garden. It may not have been the most enjoyable job and I may not have been that successful at it, but I could definitely see God's hand and timing. It taught me to overcome my fear of talking to strangers. By the end of my stint selling the tickets, I became a beast on the phone and learned how to talk to anyone.

While doing the Cubs ticket sales, I also bought myself a mower, trimmer, and blower—all the stuff that I had learned how to use back in St. Louis. I gave out flyers, cut cool designs in my yard, but no one hired me. I felt like a failure. I was so discouraged, especially after I didn't have the ticket sales job anymore. I even thought about going back to prison. I had no intention of committing a crime, but prison honestly just seemed easier. I couldn't find a job, Julie was only able to find part-time work, our house was in foreclosure, and even the insurance policy money that my mother had left me couldn't save it because the mortgage was upside down.

My mom had died. I felt at the end of my rope. I just didn't see how I was ever going to thrive on the outside. I no longer felt relevant. In prison, I had poured myself into so many things that made me feel productive and helpful. Now, I felt like I couldn't do anything to make a difference in ministry or my family. But I kept going. I had to trust that God hadn't brought me this far, done that many miracles to obtain my release, just to have me end up wasting my life.

I was still in contact with Randy, and he gave me the name of a friend of his, Bob, who lived in my area. I contacted him, and we went to breakfast. He gave me the name of guy at a church called Willow Creek, which is a massive church in Chicago. I decided to try to volunteer through them. When I initially called, the person who answered simply said that they didn't have any housing to offer. That made me a little mad because I wasn't asking for housing. I couldn't seem to even volunteer successfully. Finally, I got through to him a little clearer, and he gave me a lady's name and number at their main location. She invited me to a monthly prison and jail meeting. They met the first Saturday of every month, which happened to be the upcoming Saturday.

On November 6, 2010, I went to my first meeting. The guest speaker was a man who started a coffee company to hire former felons. His name was Pete Leonard. He started it because his brother-in-law was a felon and a genius, and couldn't get a job. He came up with the business plan to roast the top one percent of coffee in the world but hire the bottom one percent of people (or the societal perception that they were). While I sat listening to him, I thought, *This guy's going to give me job!*

After the meeting, I went up and talked to him. He gave me his card and said to come by the plant on Monday. I went and filled out the application. I was interviewed on Tuesday and was hired on Thursday. By Friday, I had started working. Immediately, I realized that God definitely has a sense of humor. I was hired on to roast the coffee—and I can't stand the smell or taste of coffee. I would literally rather clean toilets than smell coffee. There I was spending my days roasting coffee, breathing in the fragrance all day long. However, I was still so thankful for the job. While it wasn't my dream job, it did turn out that God was working toward more than simply giving Himself a laugh. This job would turn out to be the next stepping stone in overcoming any residual fear of talking to strangers.

I roasted coffee for several months, until one day I was asked to help give out samples at a major grocery store chain that allowed demos. At first, it felt like all we did was stand around waiting for people to approach us. I wondered if that was all we were allowed to do, or if we could invite people to come over and try it. They said that I could. It worked! In no time, I became really good at it, selling so much coffee. I acquired stacks of magazines to learn all about coffee and roasting. I absorbed a ton of knowledge to share at the demo. After seeing my results at the demo tables, the owner decided I should sell instead of roast. I was back in sales, but this time I excelled.

The coffee career was definitely a time of personal growth for me too. I had now talked to so many people—most of whom were strangers—from cold-calling for the Cubs to helping people realize that we had the best coffee in town at I Have a Bean Coffee Roasting Company. It was preparing me for more, though. It was all teaching me to ask, "Who's my audience?" I knew how to adapt the conversation for the audience, and not be afraid or intimidated. It also allowed me to figure out a rhythm to talking to people about my past. The demo area did not advertise that they employed former felons. However, they were open about having a three-legged stool philosophy to their business. The first leg was coffee that was fresh, roasted daily, and locally produced. The second leg was that they only used the top one percent of coffee in the world. And finally, the third leg was that they were open to hiring felons. They were the Second Chance Coffee Company.

Word did get out. Sometimes, people would ask me if I had ever been in prison, and we would talk about it. I worried there would be a lot of hostile responses, but instead most people were favorable to the idea. Many even shared how they had been touched in some way by prison. It's amazing how God even used a coffee sales job to help prepare me for talking about prison with people. I ended up working there until July 2012.

Around that time, Randy invited me to a conference at Emmaus Worldwide to share my testimony at the prison conference. I agreed, and thoroughly enjoyed the time. But at that point, I still had no thoughts of working in a prison ministry. Yet, that weekend people began asking if I'd ever thought of working for Set Free. Maybe not so coincidentally, around that same time, I was reffing basketball in the city. I met a guy from Kansas City who was helping plant a church in the Chicago suburbs. We ended up talking about the non-profit world. I had always thought that if you worked for a non-profit, you didn't get paid. It was all volunteer. But this guy opened my eyes to how it all really worked. He told me that sometimes there were paid positions, if you could raise support.

So when people asked me if I had ever thought of working for Set Free, I said that I would love to if that was an option. Someone suggested Julie and I should pray about it. We did, and we felt led to have me begin my journey back into the prisons. I accepted the offer and began raising support. Randy explained to me that usually churches won't give to the ministry, but people in the churches would. God blessed the support, which felt like a confirmation that Set Free was where I was supposed to be.

Looking back over those first few years, I can see clearly how God was preparing me all along for life in full-time ministry. When I left prison, I had no desire to do prison ministry. I wanted to work with youth to help them avoid prison, but God had other plans. Even in the darkest days, when things felt almost hopeless, God was working. He used those hundreds of cold calls, even the really awkward ones when I was trying to learn how to do it, and the discipline of showing up every day to roast coffee even as I hated the smell, and putting myself out there at the demo gig, all to refine my skill set and my mindset.

In ministry, He allows times of financial stress to teach us to trust Him and remind us that we are not in it for the money. I can see now that our financial crisis prepared me for that. Every little thing taught me something. Even the mowing business that started off so unsuccessfully taught me perseverance (a vital trait for a life of service) because I stuck with it and finally made a worthwhile little side job. It turned out that just like in prison, life on the streets is about faithfulness in the details.

We remain faithful when things don't look good from our human perspective. God is good. All the time. Life on the streets was not easy. In fact, it was so much harder than I had even anticipated, but God always has a plan. I could've never guessed that God was going to get me out of prison just to ask me to go back in.

CHAPTER 17
GOING BACK TO PRISON SET ME FREE

"Give yourself fully to God. He will use you to accomplish great things on the condition that you believe much more in His love than in your own weakness." ~Mother Teresa

Once I began officially working for Set Free full time, I dove right in—in what felt like the shallow end of the pool of the ministry. Sure, all of the things on the outside (the correspondence work, the fundraising, getting the word out about what we were doing, etc.) was vital, and, in many ways, was the heart of the ministry. But right away, it became obvious that there was one huge aspect of it that I was not allowed to do: work back inside the prisons. Unlike Randy, his kids, and other VICs, because of my parole status, I was not allowed to become a VIC. What was discouraging was that I was scheduled to be on parole until 2079! I had to wait 67 years to go back in. Now that I was fully on board with the prison ministry, I couldn't help but start to wonder what it would look like to go back into prison, especially the one I spent thirteen years in.

I talked to Randy. He said that we should pray about it and maybe wait until I'd been out for five years. I didn't like the idea of waiting another two years, but he was the one who would have to initiate the process, so it was out of my hands. As time went on, the desire to go back in got stronger, and my patience was wearing thin. I hit the five-year mark and immediately contacted Randy to ask him to get the ball rolling. Technically, there was a small chance they'd let me go back in to visit, but it wasn't likely. However, he said that he would talk to the warden in Southeast Missouri about it first, since he and I were already familiar with one another.

Days later, Randy called me. He was so excited. He said that the warden wanted me to come into his prison to talk to staff and inmates about the importance of programs in prison. I definitely could talk about that since I had taken almost every program available during my fifteen-plus years of incarceration. In fact, the warden and I met when I first took a program about victims; that's how we had gotten to know one another. He told Randy that I was a "success story," and that he wanted me to speak about how the programs benefitted me in prison and out. The reason this was so significant was because most prison staff don't believe that programs work, so they either don't allow them in their institutions, or don't put much effort into making the programs a success.

I couldn't believe it! The warden wanted me to speak to the prison *staff*! That was unheard of. I thought I was dreaming. That wasn't all. Randy told another warden about the experience at Southeast, and the other warden said that he wanted me to come into his prison too. That was even more amazing! Why? This prison was the same one that was home to me for thirteen years. That was the place where I developed my relationship with Christ and had so many encounters with God that it was crazy.

Because of the magnitude of all of this, I just knew that none of it would happen. Randy sent me a form to fill out to get the process going. I felt that I was supposed to invite some of my closest friends to accompany me, if this really did happen. I sent emails out to some people, and five responded yes. We all filled out the forms, and I sent them in. We waited. During the wait, Randy told me that the Chief of Custody at Potosi didn't want me to come into the prison. That didn't surprise me because Potosi was very security-minded. It housed the death row inmates. Yet, Randy wasn't deterred. He decided to contact a higher prison official to seek approval. That person said yes, and that he'd make sure I got in. Wow!

God's hand was all over this whole endeavor. Since all of this was coming together so smoothly, I knew that this trip was bigger than me, and I began to seek God to find out what other purposes He had in mind for the trip. I invited my friends because I knew I would need emotional support. I also thought it would be cool if they could see what prison was like on the inside. We got a date and as the days grew closer, I became more nervous. I would be reunited with brothers in Christ that I hadn't seen in many years. Some of them played a huge part in my learning how to walk with Christ. One was a father figure to me, and another was the big brother I never had. They both were examples of how to live for God and deal with prison life. There were other brothers who God used at various times in my life to teach and encourage me in my walk. It was just going to be so big that I couldn't actually believe it was going to happen.

When the day came, we all piled into the rental car and headed to St. Louis. One friend kept us occupied by asking questions the whole ride down. That helped to keep my nerves down. I think a few others may have been annoyed by it, but I thought it was funny. The guys with me all knew each other but weren't necessarily best friends. It was cool to me for them to get to know each other. A couple of them were once really good friends but because of some things that had happened, their relationship had changed. There were several dynamics taking place with all the characters aboard, and I wanted to see how God was going to impact all of us individually and collectively.

We made it to the hotel, checked in, ate, and then turned in for the night. We had to get up at 5:00 a.m. in order to begin our journey to prison. We picked up Randy, and headed to Charleston. Along the way, we discussed the rules for the institution. We also discussed the places we would be going to and who we would meet once we got inside the prison. I was excited to see some familiar faces, and to be reunited with a few brothers who were instrumental in my growth and walk with Christ.

One of those guys was Jacob. God used Jacob as an example of how to walk with Christ despite being in prison. His strength and passion for the Lord gave me the courage to be bold for Christ, no matter the outcome. Another brother was Dre. Dre was the big brother I never had. We laughed together, argued, wrestled, and even cried together. He was someone who I could ask anything, and he wouldn't judge me. He kept it real at all times. He didn't allow me to get away with anything! David was a brother who was dedicated to work for the Lord. He was the epitome of consistency. If you needed something done, he was the man. You could always count on him, and he would always come through. There were other brothers, too, who impacted my life. Some were still doing time, and some were executed over the years. Needless to say, I was eager to see those who were still there.

As we pulled up to the prison, the excitement went through the roof. I didn't know what to expect, but I wanted to run inside and see my brothers in Christ. How ironic that I had been so elated to be released, and now I was elated to go back in. It seemed to take forever to make it through the check points. Once inside, we went to the warden's office. I met him years ago when he worked as a caseworker in the other prison, while I was doing a program. He made his way up to warden.

We sat down, and he thanked me for my willingness to come into his prison and address his staff and inmate program facilitators. I thanked him for his willingness to allow this to take place. This had never been done before, and none of us really knew how it would all turn out. We left his office with an escort to take us to our next stop. Before we left, we were told that the guy escorting us had been beaten up by an inmate his first day on the job. I didn't understand why the warden would tell us that. Was it to strike fear in the hearts of my friends who had never been in a prison, or was it just to let them know that it was a dangerous place where anything could happen? I thought it was funny.

We finally got out of the office and were headed to the building where the chapel and program offices were located. We got there and I immediately saw two guys that I hadn't seen in years. They had a tripod and camera to videotape our session. I introduced them to my friends and waited for the other inmates to get there. The guys we were waiting for worked for Set Free ministries inside the prison. They did some of the same work I had done at Potosi. They finally arrived, and I saw some of my best friends. We hugged each other. The moment was surreal. I couldn't believe that was taking place. It was like a dream.

Everyone sat down, and Randy asked them to introduce themselves and tell what they did for Set Free. Each one spoke about their part in the ministry, and how it impacted their lives. It was such a blessing to see so many dedicated men who were living for the Lord and helping other men find their way to Christ. After introductions, we left, and they got to work.

My buddies, Randy, and I were then taken on tour to see where the church services were held and the library where Christian material could be checked out. Because the prison was locked down for tuberculosis shots, we weren't going to be able to visit any housing units—something I had hoped we could do. That was a big bummer. By then it was lunch time, and we decided to go out for lunch. I would've preferred the chow hall so that my friends could've gotten that experience too.

We got back after lunch, and I saw an inmate walking on the yard. Then I saw a few more walking. Was that what I thought it was? Was the prison open now? It was! I was amazed. Our escort informed us that we could go on the prison yard and then into a housing unit. I couldn't believe it. I was like a kid in a candy store. I was walking way ahead of everyone, looking for guys I recognized. We passed by the chow hall and then stepped inside the gym. I wanted my friends to see guys working out and playing ball so that they could see how all of that actually worked.

We moved on to the housing unit. Suddenly, I saw someone that I thought I knew. It looked like my "big brother" Dre, but I wasn't sure at first. As he and I got closer to one another, I saw that it was him. I began calling his name, and he looked up at me. Our eyes locked and tears began streaming down both of our faces. We hugged, and he said he had to go because he was getting too emotional. He said that he would see me later in the visiting room where the program would be held. I hadn't seen him in years.

While the day I found out that I would be paroled was an awesome day, it also meant the abrupt separation from so many guys who had become family to me. I never even got to say goodbye. Now, there I was, face-to-face with some of them again. Words can't describe the emotions that were playing out inside me.

The group and I proceeded into the housing unit. Then something completely amazing happened. Our escort got the door opened to the dorm, and we went right on in. WHAT?! My friends and I were standing inside the dorm room where the guys lived. There were inmates all around. Some were on the phone, a few playing cards, and some just hanging out talking. I immediately saw a guy who used to live next door to me—a neighbor. We hugged and began talking. I had never actually been incarcerated at this prison—Southeast Correctional Center. But with transfers, there were so many guys I knew.

He started naming off people I knew who lived in that dorm. I told him to get all of them! He started calling out people's names, and they started coming out of their cells. I don't know what my friends were doing at that point, but I started seeing more guys, shaking hands, and hugging brothers in Christ. They were all glad to see me, and told me how proud they were of me. I almost lost it. Most of these guys were never getting out. They told me I was their hope! I couldn't wrap my mind around that. Me, Louis Dooley, was someone's hope. What a humbling thing to hear. It motivated me then and still motivates me now to continue the journey the Lord has set before me.

After the housing unit, we made our way to see Jacob, my spiritual "father figure." He worked in the prison's laundry. We waited outside the door for him to come out. As Jacob came out, we locked eyes. It was like our spirits reunited. We gave each other a huge hug as tears streamed down our faces. It was such a blessing to see him after all those years. I asked him how he had been, and of course he said that he was blessed. He stated that he was in his thirty-sixth year of incarceration and that God was still able to deliver him. His exact words were, "If God can part the Red Sea, He could open the prison gates for me." If there was one word I would use to describe Jacob, it would be *faithful*. Since I first met him over twenty years ago, he was still strong in his faith. Before we left, Jacob asked if he could pray for us. He placed his hand on my shoulder and began to pray. A friend of mine who was with us later said that his prayer was so powerful that it was like lightning shooting from his mouth.

On that high note, we left for the visiting room where I would be addressing some prison staff, as well as inmate program facilitators. As the inmates began coming in, I saw more old faces that I hadn't seen in years. We greeted each other and started catching up before the program began. Everyone arrived, and we were seated. The warden began telling everyone the reason why we were all there. He stated that most prison staff don't believe programs work. He wanted them to hear how programs benefited me inside and outside of prison. I got up and delivered my speech. God showed me grace once again. I felt that it was the best speech I'd ever delivered. Several prison staff came up to me afterward and told me that after hearing me, their mindset had changed. Wow! I couldn't believe that something I said changed the mindset of a person.

I shook hands with all of my Christian brothers as they went back to their cells. It was a somber moment. They were encouraged by the talk and encouraged me to keep serving the Lord and doing His work.

We left the prison, but a part of me remained there with my brothers. We took a few pictures outside of the prison. As we were on the road back to the hotel, Randy told us that he had gone to the warden's office. The warden was crying because of how impactful the afternoon was. It was another amazing thing to cap off an amazing day. I was exhausted like I had never been before. It wasn't physical, but emotional. That was just the first day.

The next day we would be visiting the prison where I spent thirteen years of my life. That visit was going to be very different than Monday's. We were going to be celebrating the twenty-year anniversary of Set Free Ministries, which started an office in the prison. Several other volunteers for Set Free were going too. As part of the celebration, we were going to bring in pizza, sub sandwiches, and donuts. That was going to be a huge treat for the men. The inmates coming to the celebration were the workers for Set Free who were incarcerated at Potosi. The big part about that prison visit was that my friends were going to get to have lunch with some of the best friends I've ever had. Some of them were even on Missouri's death row.

The first time I came to Potosi, I was a twenty-year-old in shackles. Now I was forty years old and a free man! The guys were awaiting our arrival in the prison's visiting room. I had so many memories of that visiting room. There were times I laughed, was afraid, even wept in that visiting room. I could remember being an inmate waiting on a visit to come. Sometimes, I would get to the actual visiting room before my visitors. I would sit and watch the door they would come through. Every time the doors opened, I would be looking for them. That was the norm for everyone waiting on their visitor.

However, this time I was on the other side of the door, waiting to go into the room. As soon as the door opened, everyone looked my way. I then knew how it felt for someone to be waiting for me. I went inside the room, and shook everyone's hands and hugged them. I had been informed beforehand not to hug, but I couldn't help it. The first guy pulled me in and wrapped his arms around me. Seeing those old faces really blessed my heart.

There were a few new faces too. A couple of the men weren't Christians when I had left. They had since given their lives to Christ. What a blessing that was to see. One guy even apologized to me. He said that he was sorry for how he spoke to and treated us Christians. I told him that no apology was needed. The fact that he'd given his life to Christ was apology enough. Everyone who came with me sat at different tables with the inmates. After a few minutes, I looked around and saw all of my friends from the outside fellowshipping with my friends on the inside. What a beautiful sight to behold!

We all started eating and just enjoyed our time together. After eating, we began passing out certificates to the men for their faithful work with Set Free Ministries along with the outside VICs who had come. We called up each person and stated how many years they had been with Set Free. I could see the pride in each person's face for their accomplishment. It wasn't self-seeking, self-glorifying pride, but a godly kind of pride. A pride that said, "Unto you O God have I committed my time and life in helping others learn of You and Your Word."

A few men shared their testimonies of how God and Set Free helped change their lives. I was blessed to share, as well. I encouraged the men to continue holding on—I knew life times get rough sometimes, and we want to throw in the towel. But we must persevere. We must continue to be diligent in the work the Lord has called us to do. I reminded them that after this work, we have heaven to look forward to for eternity.

We said our goodbyes. I left feeling that I would be back one day. It was another emotionally draining day. I was so overjoyed that five of my closest brothers were able to share that experience with me. Their support was a blessing. We began making our way back to Chicago.

We had many hours for each one of us to debrief about the whole experience. It was cool how each person took away something different. It was kind of like the four gospels—each person saw it from a different perspective. I was excited to get back home and share this experience with my wife. I really would have liked her to meet my brothers inside, too, but I felt that God wanted me to invite those men for the first trip.

Since the trip, an advisory board was created to help me stay on track with the various jobs and interests I have. They provide accountability, which is so critical to success on the streets for a former inmate.

A couple of days passed, and life went back to normal. I was out mowing some lawns and doing some fall clean-up for my little side job. My phone rang. It was my parole officer. I answered the call, expecting him to ask me when I was going to be home so we could have our monthly meeting. Instead, he asked me how my trip was. I told him that it went very well and thanked him again for his part in helping to make it happen. (I had to get his initial approval.) He then asked me if "they" said anything to me while I was there. I said no, even though I didn't know who "they" were or what "it" was that they would've said to me. He asked me if I said "anything." I said no again, not knowing what "anything" was or "who" I would've said it to. I was thinking to myself, *What the heck is going on?* I was getting kind of nervous.

He paused and said, "I don't understand this." He paused again before adding, "This just doesn't make any sense." He paused again.

By that point, I was getting frustrated and worried. I asked, "What's going on?"

My parole officer read a letter he had received from the Missouri Department of Corrections. The letter stated that they had released me from parole, and they were telling the state of Illinois that they no longer had to monitor me for them.

I couldn't believe it. I just kept saying, "This is crazy! This is crazy!" It was 2014. My parole was originally slated to go until 2079. The state of Missouri had initiated ending my parole sixty-five years early! The letter didn't even list a reason for the decision. Once again, something I may never know.

I got off the phone with him and called my wife. Her response was, "Stop playing."

I told her that I wasn't! The first thing that came to my mind was that in that moment, I was freer than I had ever been in my entire life. I was born into the bondage of sin, just like everyone else.[1] Shortly after my conviction, I gave my life to Christ and sin's bondage was broken[2] in my life, but I was physically in bondage because I was in prison. After fifteen-and-a-half years in prison, I was freed from the physical part of prison but was on parole until 2079. I was still connected to the state of Missouri. But in that moment—with that news—I was released from parole and was TOTALLY FREE! Praise God!

God had already done some amazing things for me by releasing me from prison early. He allowed me to go into two maximum security prisons while still on parole. Then to top it off, He released me from parole. God is good, and I don't know why He loves me so much. I am truly humbled and in awe of His grace, power, and love. I am confident that God loves us all and wants to be as big a part of our lives as we allow Him. As weak and frail a man as I am and God blessed me too, how much more so He wants to bless those who are faithful and diligently seek Him.[3]

The story that God is writing in my life isn't over. It's just beginning. I have no doubt that God did not work these miracles for me to squander my freedom. He has plans for me. If I stayed on parole, those visits would most likely have been the only visits I ever made inside an institution. I would've been forced to work for Set Free solely from the outside. I had served God so many years behind those iron doors, but upon release, those doors were closed to me. Now, I was free to walk back into prison and serve again.

EPILOGUE
THE JOURNEY CONTINUES

"I am not a finisher...I am a blazer of trails. Others must take up the various trails of truth and carry them on."
~George Washington Carver
"God, let me make a difference for you that is utterly disproportionate to who I am." ~Norman Geisler

What does a person do once he's witnessed multiple miracles of biblical proportions on his behalf? I can't speak for everyone, but me, I dove right in to anything and everything I could. It suddenly felt like there was no ceiling on what God could and just might accomplish through me if I kept myself a willing vessel. I had such a heart for so many things, though. Yes, prison ministry was a big one. But my heart was for all people. I desperately wanted to help youth. Prison saved my life, but clearly the logical preference is to avoid prison. If I could help even one kid avoid that road, I would do everything in my power to do so.

I also looked around and saw the frustrating cycle of poor neighborhoods. Fathers leaving an inheritance of violence, drugs, and abandonment to their children. In my mind, there had to be a solution for that too. My eyes looked out even further and saw a world crippled by evil and even deeper poverty than that found in the United States. People who were without access to the gospel or hope. Again, I felt a tug.

Sometimes, my biggest enemy is my own heart's burden for so many people. Where do I start? Where SHOULD I start? I knew I couldn't do everything. I'm not even supposed to. But I knew I was supposed to do something. So I prayed. I talked with friends, mentors, Julie. Then I prayed some more. While clearly continuing with Set Free was a big one, I began simply keeping my eyes and mind open to opportunities as God presented them. In no time, just like He had done for the prison doors, God was opening doors all over the country and the world to share my testimony. He even made a way for me to speak in public high schools in Seattle and Chicago! I went to Kosovo and Albania in July 2015, then Haiti in February 2016. I spoke at so many churches and conferences and continue to do so. Sometimes, it is still slightly surreal that me, Louis Dooley, just a kid from East St. Louis, now has such opportunities to serve in so many places. I have even done a few TV and newspaper interviews.

My days now never look quite the same from week to week, but much of my time is spent doing Bible studies in Cook County Jail, mentoring others, working with people getting out of prison or jail, men's Bible studies, Bible studies at Southeast (the prison where I gave my speech to prison staff back in 2014), working with the correspondence aspect of Set Free for the state of Illinois, and squeezing in a game of basketball when time permits. My love of sports didn't end upon release after all.

When asked where I see myself in five years, I don't really know. I see so many things. I want to help make Set Free Ministries an even bigger ministry—help it to grow, and get the funding it needs to do so. I would love to see more offices opened in prisons. Maybe someday I'll pastor a church. I would love to get a movement going where people who don't have to live in the ghetto choose to move to the ghetto to start helping create a more positive environment and sense of community. I want to keep helping with youth.

Basically, I just want to keep being used by God. Life is not easy even now. Even being off parole, my past is still my past. I work in ministry, and unlike those televangelists you see on TV, I am not in this to make money so I can have my own private plane. I will probably spend the rest of my life in a position where I have to trust God to provide financially from month to month. If that's the case, that's just fine.

I don't know what the future holds. No one does. I can think and plan and envision. Only God knows which of those things will actually come to fruition. I guess in the end, I just want to live a life that people look at and see that there is always hope through faith in the love of God, and the work of His Son on the cross for each of us. Everyone was designed by God for a purpose. Everyone has a chance. It is about our choice to hear His call. No matter how dark a day or a year or a life seems, there is a Light waiting for you to want Him. He already wants you.

NOTES

CHAPTER 1
1. Luke 12:5; Romans 6:23
2. Romans 3:23
3. John 3:16
4. Ephesians 2:8-10
5. 2 Corinthians 5:10; Hebrews 9:27
6. Ephesians 1:7; Acts 13:38-39; Acts 26:18
7. 2 Corinthians 5:17

CHAPTER 2
1. Luke 6:27-36

CHAPTER 5
1. Matthew 5:39
2. Romans 12:19; Deuteronomy 32:35
3. John 15:20; John 13:16; Matthew 10:24; Matthew 5:11,12; Luke 6:23; Isaiah 53-3-12

CHAPTER 6
1. Romans 2:4; Numbers 32:23; Revelation 3:19

CHAPTER 7

1. 2 Samuel 11
2. 2 Samuel 12:1-14
3. 2 Samuel 12:15-23
4. Hebrews 12:6-11; Proverbs 3:12
5. 2 Samuel 12:24-25; Matthew 1:6, 17; Luke 3:31
6. Romans 6:1-2

CHAPTER 9

1. Ephesians 6:19-20
2. Psalm 138:3

CHAPTER 10

1. 2 Corinthians 5:17

CHAPTER 12

1. Matthew 5:44

CHAPTER 17

1. Romans 3:23
2. Romans 6
3. Hebrews 11:6